THE TEAHOUSE
OF THE AUGUST MOON

Other Plays by John Patrick

THE WILLOW AND I

THE HASTY HEART

THE STORY OF MARY SURRATT

THE CURIOUS SAVAGE

LO AND BEHOLD

THE WRESTLING MATCH FROM ACT III

The Teahouse
of the August Moon

A Play by
JOHN PATRICK [pseud.]

Adapted from the Novel
by Vern Sneider

G. P. Putnam's Sons
New York

FOR

BILL MYERS

*Our Organic Commander
Who Gave Us
The Moon With
A Snap of His Fingers.*

The Teahouse of the August Moon opened at the Martin Beck Theatre in New York City on October 15, 1953. It was produced by Maurice Evans in association with George Schaefer and was directed by Robert Lewis. The production was designed by Peter Larkin with costumes by Noel Taylor. The cast, in order of appearance, was as follows:

SAKINI	*David Wayne*
SERGEANT GREGOVICH	*Harry Jackson*
COL. WAINWRIGHT PURDY III	*Paul Ford*
CAPTAIN FISBY	*John Forsythe*
OLD WOMAN	*Naoe Kondo*
OLD WOMAN'S DAUGHTER	*Mara Kim*
THE DAUGHTER'S CHILDREN	*Moy Moy Thom, Joyce Chen and Kenneth Wong*
LADY ASTOR	*Saki*
ANCIENT MAN	*Kame Ishikawa*
MR. HOKAIDA	*Chuck Morgan*
MR. OMURA	*Kuraji Seida*
MR. SUMATA	*Kaie Deei*
MR. SUMATA'S FATHER	*Kikuo Hiromura*
MR. SEIKO	*Haim Winant*
MISS HIGA JIGA	*Shizu Moriya*
MR. KEORA	*Yuki Shimoda*
MR. OSHIRA	*William Hansen*
VILLAGERS	*Jerry Fujikawa, Frank Ogawa, Richard Akagi, Laurence Kim and Norman Chi*
LADIES' LEAGUE FOR DEMOCRATIC ACTION	*Vivian Thom, Naoe Kondo, Mary Ann Reeve and Mara Kim*
LOTUS BLOSSOM	*Mariko Niki*
CAPTAIN MC LEAN	*Larry Gates*

ACT I

ACT II

ACT III

ACT ONE

Scene I

Directly behind the house curtain is a second curtain consisting of four panels of split bamboo. Each of these sections can be raised and lowered individually.

AT RISE: *As the house lights dim, the Oriental strains from a stringed instrument can be heard playing softly in the background. A pool of light picks up* SAKINI *standing framed against the bamboo backing. He wears a pair of tattered shorts and a native shirt. His shoes, the gift of a G.I., are several sizes too large. His socks are also too large and hang in wrinkles over his ankles. He is an Okinawan who might be any age between thirty and sixty. In repose his face betrays age, but the illusion is shattered quickly by his smile of childlike candor.*

With hands together in prayer-like supplication, he walks down to the footlights and bows to the audience center in solemn ritual. Then he bows from the waist—to the left and to the right.

Straightening up, he examines the audience seated before him with open curiosity. The music ceases. As it ceases, SAKINI *begins to work his jaws vigorously.*

SAKINI
Tootie-fruitie.
(*He takes the gum from his mouth and, wrapping it carefully in a piece of paper, puts it in a matchbox and restores it to a pocket in his shirt.*)

7

Most generous gift of American sergeant.

    (*He resumes his original posture of dignity.*)

Lovely ladies, kind gentlemen:

Please to introduce myself.

Sakini by name.

Interpreter by profession.

Education by ancient dictionary.

Okinawan by whim of gods.

History of Okinawa reveal distinguished record of conquerors.

We have honor to be subjugated in fourteenth century by Chinese pirates.

In sixteenth century by English missionaries.

In eighteenth century by Japanese war lords.

And in twentieth century by American Marines.

Okinawa very fortunate.

Culture brought to us. . . . Not have to leave home for it.

Learn many things.

Most important that rest of world not like Okinawa.

World filled with delightful variation.

Illustration.

In Okinawa . . . no locks on doors.

Bad manners not to trust neighbors.

In America . . . lock and key big industry.

Conclusion?

Bad manners good business.

In Okinawa . . . wash self in public bath with nude lady quite proper.

Picture of nude lady in private home . . . quite improper.

In America . . . statue of nude lady in park win prize.

But nude lady in flesh in park win penalty.

Conclusion?

Pornography question of geography.

But Okinawans most eager to be educated by conquerors.

Deep desire to improve friction.

Not easy to learn.

Sometimes painful.

But pain makes man think.
Thought makes man wise.
Wisdom makes life endurable.
So ...
(*He crosses back to the left of the first of the panels.*)
We tell little story to demonstrate splendid example of benevolent assimilation of democracy by Okinawa.
(*He claps his hands, signaling the stagehand to raise the first of the four panels. Flush against the curtain is revealed a sign nailed onto a denuded palm stump. It points toward the other side of the stage and reads: COL. WAINRIGHT PURDY III.*)
Boss by name of Colonel Purdy—Three. Number three after name indicate he is a son of a son of a son.
(*He steps to the next panel and claps again. The screen rolls up revealing a laundry line tied to a second denuded stump. As these panels are raised the background is revealed in sections. It includes a jeep parked against a pile of empty gasoline drums, trees ripped of foliage by recent gunfire—all creating an impression of general destruction. There are several articles of wearing apparel hanging on the laundry line, foremost of which is a pair of khaki pants size forty.*)
Colonel Purdy, Three, displays splendid example of cleanliness for native population to follow. But native population cannot follow. Native not *have* two pairs of pants.
(*He then claps for the next screen to rise, revealing more of the laundry. To the extreme right is seen the outside of Colonel Purdy's Quonset office. Nailed on the post holding the other end of the line is a sign reading: OFFICERS' LAUNDRY ONLY.*)
Colonel Purdy put up many signs. This exceedingly civilized. Make it very easy for uncivilized to know what *not* to do. Here laundry of officer not to fraternize with laundry of enlisted man.
(SAKINI *now signals for the last panel to be raised, reveal-*

ing the inside of the hut. Colonel Purdy's vacant desk is beside the door. A sign denotes his proprietorship. Another sign admonishes the visitor to THINK! *The office is small and sparse. A bulletin board for "Daily Orders" hangs on the upstage wall. Against this wall is the desk of Sergeant Gregovich. Behind a sign denoting his rating sits the* SERGEANT. *His posture is frozen—as if awaiting a signal to come to life.* SAKINI *crosses down center to explain to his audience.*)

This gentleman honorable Sergeant Gregovich—assistant to Colonel Purdy. Not son of a son of a son.

(*He turns toward the* SERGEANT.)

Play has begun, Sergeant.

(GREGOVICH *now comes to life. He begins to chew his gum vigorously and to look about the office. He rises and crosses down to Colonel Purdy's desk. He gets down on his hands and knees in front of the desk and reaches under it.*)

Oh, you know what he is doing? Explanation. Colonel Purdy great student of history. Every month wife of Colonel Purdy send him magazine called *Adventure Magazine.* Cover has picture of pirate with black patch over eye. Everybody try to steal magazine. Colonel hide under desk so he can read first.

(GREGOVICH *rises triumphantly with the magazine.*)

But Sergeant always find. Smart mouse.

(GREGOVICH *returns to his desk and buries himself behind the pages of the magazine. At this point* COLONEL PURDY *himself enters from the left. As his laundry has indicated, he is a man of proportions. The worries of the world in general and the Army of Occupation in particular weigh heavily on his shoulders. He stops to glance at the nearest official sign. He takes out a small notebook to make an entry. Sakini's presence is not recognized until indicated.*)

This gentleman exalted boss—Colonel Purdy, Three. Subject of sovereign American city of Pottawattamie, Michigan.

(COLONEL PURDY *hiccups and taps his chest.*)

Also subject to indignity of indigestion. Colonel Purdy explain this by saying—

PURDY

> (*Clears his throat and says to himself*)
> An occupational disorder of the Army of Occupation.
> (*He taps his chest again and puts the notebook away.*)

SAKINI

Colonel Purdy very wise man. Always hit nail on head.
Every morning, look at sky—
> (COLONEL PURDY *puts his hands on his hips and glances skyward.*)
And make prophecy.

PURDY

It's not going to rain today.

SAKINI

And you know what? Not rain. Of course, not rain here this time of year in whole history of Okinawa. But Colonel not make mistake.
> (COLONEL PURDY *goes down the laundry line and stops to button the top of a pair of shorts.*)
Colonel Purdy gentleman of propriety.
> (PURDY *goes back to count articles of clothing.*)
And precision. Always count laundry.

PURDY

> (*Counts aloud*)
> Un—deux—trois.

SAKINI

Explanation. Army teach Colonel French for invasion of Europe. Then send to Okinawa instead.

11

PURDY
... quatre—cinq—six—sept.
(*He beams with satisfaction.*)

SAKINI
Very good. Colonel count in French and not notice one pair shorts missing in Okinawa.

PURDY
(*His expression quickly changes.*)
What?
(*He goes down the line and counts again in English.*)
One, two, three, four, five, six, seven!
(*He inhales deeply for an explosion.*)

SAKINI
(*Rushes down to the footlights*)
Oh—ladies please close ears unless want to hear unladylike oath.
(*He puts his hands over his own ears.*)

PURDY
(*Explodes*)
Damitohell! Damitohell! Damitohell!

SAKINI
Now Colonel yell loud for Sakini. But Sakini hide. Pretend to be asleep.
(*He promptly curls up on the ground beside the office, with his back to the* COLONEL.)

PURDY
Sakini!
(SAKINI *snores.* PURDY *strides over to tower above him.*)
Sakini!

SAKINI

> (*Rises quickly*)

Oh—oh. Good morning, boss. You sure surprise me.

PURDY

Where is the boy that does my laundry!

SAKINI

Bring laundry back and go home to sleep, boss.

PURDY

I want you to find out why my laundry comes back every week with one piece missing!

SAKINI

Gets lost, boss.

PURDY

I *know* it gets lost. What I want to find out is *how* it gets lost.

SAKINI

Very simple. Boy takes laundry to top of mountain stream and throws in water. Then runs down hill fast as dickens to catch laundry at bottom. Sometimes not run fast enough.

PURDY

> (*Heaves a martyr's sigh*)

No wonder you people were subjugated by the Japanese. If you're not sleeping you're running away from work. Where is your "get-up-and-go"?

SAKINI

Guess "get-up-and-go" went.

> (SAKINI *starts to sit on the ground.*)

PURDY

Well, get up and go over to the mess and see if Captain Fisby has arrived. If he has, tell him to report to me at once. Hurry!
(*As* SAKINI *starts across the stage* PURDY *looks with annoyance at the G.I. socks that hang down over Sakini's ankles.*)
Sakini!

SAKINI

(*Stops*)
Yes, boss?

PURDY

You're a civilian employee in the pay of the United States Army. And should dress accordingly. *Pull Your Socks Up!*

SAKINI

Yes, boss.
(*He leans over and pulls up his socks—not a great improvement.*)
Anything else, boss?

PURDY

That will be all.
(SAKINI *ambles across the stage so slowly that the* COLONEL *explodes in exasperation.*)
Is that as *fast* as you can walk!

SAKINI

Oh no, boss. But if walk any faster—socks fall down.
(*As* SAKINI *exits,* COLONEL PURDY *closes his eyes and counts to ten in vehement French.* PURDY *remains arrested in this position.* SAKINI *re-enters downstage. He signals the closing of the panels left, shutting out the* COLONEL.)

SAKINI

Introduction now over. Kindly direct attention to office.

(*He leans out toward the footlights and calls across stage.*)

Oh, Honorable Sergeant—ready now to continue.

(SERGEANT GREGOVICH *again comes to life. He glances out the office door and quickly hides the* Adventure Magazine. *He stands at attention as* COLONEL PURDY *enters.* SAKINI *exits into the wings.*)

GREGOVICH

Good morning, sir.

PURDY

At ease.

(COLONEL PURDY *sits down behind his desk and begins searching through the papers on it.*)

I'm thinking of getting rid of that interpreter. He doesn't set a good example.

GREGOVICH

We've got to have someone around that speaks the language, sir.

PURDY

You're quite right, Sergeant. You're quite right. It isn't often I make a mistake, but when I do—

GREGOVICH

It's a beaut?

PURDY

(*Stiffly*)

I wasn't going to say that. I was going to say— I admit it.

GREGOVICH
Sorry, sir.

PURDY
We've got a new officer reporting this morning. He's been transferred to us from "Psychological Warfare."
(*Benevolently*)
I don't suppose you happen to know who *they* are?

GREGOVICH
Aren't they something at the rear of the Rear Echelon?

PURDY
They're just the cream of the Army's geniuses. They're just the brains behind the fighting heart. Every man jack of them has a mind like a steel trap. And we are lucky to be getting one of their officers.

GREGOVICH
I'll watch my step, sir.

PURDY
While we're waiting for Captain Fisby, I want you to make a note of some new signs I want painted.

GREGOVICH
(*Takes up a pad*)
The painter hasn't finished the ones you ordered yesterday, sir.

PURDY
There's only one answer to that. Put on another sign painter. Now. I noticed the men were dancing with each other in the canteen the other night.

GREGOVICH

Yes, sir.

> (*He writes on his pad*)

"No dancing allowed."

PURDY

> (*Annoyed*)

I didn't say that, Gregovich! I don't object to the men dancing. I want them to enjoy themselves. But it doesn't set a good example for the natives to see noncoms dancing with enlisted men. So have a sign posted saying, "Sergeants Are Forbidden to Dance with Privates."

GREGOVICH

Yes, sir.

PURDY

Have another sign put up beside that clear pool of water just below the falls—"For Officers Only."

GREGOVICH

Where will the men bathe, sir?

PURDY

There is another pool just below it they can use.

GREGOVICH

If you'll pardon me, sir—they're not going to like that. They'll be bathing in water the officers have already bathed in.

PURDY

That's a valid objection, Gregovich. We don't want to do anything unreasonable.

> (*He concentrates for a moment.*)

How far is the second pool below the first?

GREGOVICH

About three hundred yards.

PURDY

(*Satisfied*)

Then it's quite all right. Water purifies itself every two hundred feet.

GREGOVICH

Do you think that will satisfy the men, sir?

PURDY

I don't see why it shouldn't. It satisfies science. Well, you might as well take those memos to the sign painter now.

GREGOVICH

Yes, sir.

(*He goes out. As soon as he is gone,* COLONEL PURDY *moves around to the front of his desk and feels under it for his* Adventure Magazine. *When he fails to find it, he kneels down on all fours to peer under the desk.* SAKINI *enters and looks around. He steps over and taps the nearest part of Colonel Purdy—his ample rear end.*)

SAKINI

Sakini here, boss.

PURDY

(*Glances around indignantly*)

Don't *ever* put your finger on an officer!

SAKINI

Not right, boss?

18

PURDY

No! If you want to announce your presence—knock!
> (*He peers under the desk again.*)

Can't you natives learn anything about custom?
> (SAKINI *stands unhappily a moment, then leans forward and knocks gently on the* COLONEL. PURDY *rises in wrath.*)

What do you think you're doing?

SAKINI

Not know, boss. Do what you ask.

PURDY

> (*Moves behind his desk*)

Everything in this Godforsaken country conspires to annoy me.
> (*He turns to* SAKINI.)

Well, where is Captain Fisby?

SAKINI

> (*Points out the door*)

He come now. I run ahead.
> (*He points to his ankles.*)

Socks fall down.
> (*He then steps back to allow* CAPTAIN FISBY *to enter.* CAPTAIN FISBY *is in his late twenties, nice-looking and rather on the earnest side. He is nervous and eager to make a good impression. He salutes smartly.*)

CAPTAIN FISBY

Captain Fisby reporting, sir.

PURDY

> (*Returns the salute*)

Welcome to Team 147, Captain.
> (*He puts out his hand.*)

FISBY

> (*Shakes hands*)

Thank you, sir.

PURDY

I can't tell you how glad I am to have you, Captain. Frankly, we're so desperate for officer personnel I'd be glad to see you even if you had two heads.

> (SAKINI *breaks into gales of laughter.* PURDY *turns to him icily.*)

That will be all, Sakini. You can wait outside.

SAKINI

> (*Bows*)

I sit by door. Not sleep!

> (*He exits.*)

PURDY

Sit down, Captain, sit down.

> (FISBY *sits facing* PURDY.)

Have you unpacked?

FISBY

> (*Proudly*)

⌈Yes *sir!* I got in last night and unpacked at once.⌋

PURDY

Well, that's too bad, because you'll have to pack again. I'm sending you to Tobiki at once. We need a man of your caliber up there right away.

> (*He laughs with forced heartiness.*)

FISBY

> (*Forces a laugh in return*)

⌈Thank you.⌋

PURDY

I'm informed, Captain, that you requested this transfer from "Psychological Warfare" to *my* outfit. May I say that I am honored.

FISBY

⌐Well—in all fairness, sir—I think I should tell you⌐ . . the information is only partly true.

PURDY

(*Pauses*)
You *didn't* request this transfer to me?

FISBY

I was *requested* to request it, sir.

PURDY

Oh.
(*He blinks to aid his digestion of this information.*)
May I ask why?

FISBY

Well, my propaganda to undermine enemy morale always seemed to undermine the staff's morale instead, sir.

PURDY

How did you get into "Psychological Warfare" in the *first* place?

FISBY

I had been requested to request a transfer.

PURDY

From what?

FISBY

Paymaster General's office.

PURDY

What was your duty there?

FISBY

I was in charge of the payroll computation machine until—
until—
> (*He flounders unhappily.*)

PURDY

Until *what?*

FISBY

Well, sir, machines have always been my mortal enemies. I don't think they're inanimate at all. I think they're full of malice and ill will. They—

PURDY

I *asked* you what happened, Captain.

FISBY

Well, this computation machine made a mistake of a quarter of a million dollars on the payroll. Unfortunately, the men were paid *before* the mistake was discovered.

PURDY

What did they do to you?

FISBY

For a while I was given a job licking envelopes.

PURDY

Then you asked for a transfer?

FISBY

No, sir, I developed an allergy to glue.

PURDY

How many outfits in this man's army have you been in, Captain?

FISBY

How many are there, sir?

PURDY

Never mind. I admit disappointment but not defeat. I'd thought you were given to me in recognition of my work here. Frankly, I expect to be made a general soon, and I want that star for my wife's crown. Naturally, that's very hush-hush.

FISBY

(*Nods*)
Naturally. Maybe I just wasn't cut out to be a soldier.

PURDY

Captain, none of us was cut out to be a soldier. But we do the job. We adjust. We adapt. We roll with the punch and bring victory home in our teeth. Do you know what *I* was before the war?

FISBY

(*Hesitates unhappily*)
A football coach?

PURDY

I was the Purdy Paper Box Company of Pottawattamie. What did I know about foreigners? But my job is to teach these natives the meaning of democracy, and they're going to learn democracy if I have to shoot every one of them.

FISBY

I'm sure your wife wouldn't want her star that way, sir.

PURDY

What did you do before the war?

FISBY

I was an associate professor at Muncie.

PURDY

What did you teach?

FISBY

The humanities.

PURDY

Captain, you are finally getting a job you're qualified by training to handle—teaching these natives how to act human.

FISBY

The humanities isn't quite that, sir.

PURDY

If you can teach one thing you can teach another. Your job at Tobiki will be to teach the natives democracy and make them self-supporting. Establish some sort of industry up there.

FISBY

Is there a general plan?

PURDY

There is a specific plan.
(*He extends a document the size of a telephone book.*)
Washington has drawn up full instructions pertaining to the welfare and recovery of these native villages. *This* is Plan B. Consider it your *Bible*, Captain.

FISBY

I'll study it carefully, sir. There might be some questions I'd like to ask you.

PURDY

(*Points to Plan B*)
Washington has anticipated all your questions.

FISBY

But I was thinking—

PURDY

You don't even have to think, Captain. This document relieves you of that responsibility.

FISBY

But in dealing with the natives, sir—

PURDY

(*Interrupts*)
It's all covered in Section Four: "Orienting the Oriental." How is your Luchuan?

FISBY

I don't know, sir. What is it?

PURDY

It's the native dialect. Well, I can see you'll need an interpreter.
(*His eyes light up and he slaps his desk.*)
I have just the man for you!
(*He turns and calls out the door.*)
Sakini!

FISBY

I could study the dialect, sir.

25

PURDY

No need. We won the war. I'll give you my own interpreter.

FISBY

Oh, I wouldn't want to deprive you of—

PURDY

I insist.
> (SAKINI *enters. He bows—and then remembers. He leans forward and politely knocks on the desk.*)

SAKINI

Sakini present. Socks up. Not sleeping.

PURDY

Sakini, this is Captain Fisby.

FISBY

Hello, Sakini.

SAKINI

> (*Bows, then turns to* PURDY)
We meet already.
> (*He smiles in comradeship.*)
You forget, boss?

PURDY

> (*Covers his face, counts to ten, then looks up*)
I am assigning you to Captain Fisby. He's going to take charge of a village at the top of Okinawa—a village called Tobiki.

SAKINI

Oh! Tobiki very nice place, boss. But not at top of Okinawa. At bottom.

26

PURDY

Don't tell me where the villages under my command are located. I happen to have looked at the map.

SAKINI

So sorry, boss. But I happen to get born in Tobiki. Is at bottom.

PURDY

(*Whips a map out of his desk*)
Then it's time you learned where you were born. I also happen to give a course in map reading.

SAKINI

(*Looks at map*)
So sorry, boss. But map upside down.

FISBY

(*Looks at map*)
He's right.

PURDY

(*Looks at map—turns it around*)
Why in hell doesn't the Army learn how to draw a map properly!
(*Turns to* SAKINI)
That will be all, Sakini. Find Sergeant Gregovich and have him assign a jeep to Captain Fisby. Then load supplies and the captain's gear in the jeep. You will be leaving at once. I'll send rice rations later.

SAKINI

(*Takes the colonel's hand and pumps it*)
Oh, thank you, boss. You very kind to send me home. I mention you in prayer to gods.
(*He turns to* FISBY.)

27

I wait at jeep for you, Captain.
> (*He starts to run, then slows down quickly.*)
Very happy, sir. Socks up.
> (*He goes out.* PURDY *turns wearily to* FISBY.)

PURDY

I sometimes think we Occupation Teams have it tougher than combat troops.
> (*He quickly holds up a protesting hand.*)
Granted they have it rough for a while. But we have the killing daily grind, with no glory in it.

FISBY

Yes, sir, I know what you mean. Life itself is a battlefield with its own obscure heroes.

PURDY

> (*Looks at* FISBY *with surprise*)
I consider that poetry, Captain.

FISBY

I'm afraid it's just prose, sir. And it isn't mine, it's Victor Hugo's.

PURDY

> (*Corrected*)
Oh, yes. Victor Hugo! How I loved *Tale of Two Cities*.

FISBY

Isn't that Dickens, sir?

PURDY

I guess I was thinking of the movie. Well! To get back to Tobiki. Your first job when you get there will be to establish a municipal government and build a school.

FISBY

A school?

PURDY

It's all in Plan B. I'll see that cement and lumber are sent down to you. Plan B calls for the schoolhouse to be pentagon-shaped.

FISBY

If you say so, sir.

PURDY

When the school is built, you will organize a Ladies' League for Democratic Action. You will deliver a series of lectures on democracy as outlined in the outline. Captain, this is a chance for you to make a name for yourself.

FISBY

I will, sir. You see, I feel that I've personally delayed victory at least a year, and I have to vindicate myself.

PURDY

That's the kind of talk I like to hear from my officers. Well, I won't detain you then.
(*He rises.*)
My only order to you is: Put that village on the map.

FISBY

Yes, sir.

PURDY

Send me a bimonthly Progress Report—in triplicate.

FISBY

Yes, sir.

PURDY
Don't duplicate your work.

FISBY
No, sir.

PURDY
Fire those natives with the Spirit of Occupation.

FISBY
Yes, sir.

PURDY
And remember—that the eyes of Washington are on our Occupation Teams. And the eyes of the world are on Washington.

FISBY
I'll keep the eyes in mind, sir.

PURDY
Good-bye, Captain.
> (FISBY *salutes smartly and goes out.* PURDY *stands for a moment, moved by the vastness of the canvas. Then he turns to his desk.*)

Where the hell is my *Adventure Magazine!*

THE SCENE BLACKS OUT QUICKLY

Scene 2

SCENE: *Outside Captain Fisby's quarters.*

TIME: *Few minutes later.*

AT RISE: CAPTAIN FISBY *and* SAKINI *enter from left and cross before the panels, all of which are now down.*

SAKINI

Everything all ready, boss. We go to Tobiki now?

FISBY

I guess so. Well, wish me luck, Sakini. I'm going out to spread the gospel of Plan B.

SAKINI

You already lucky, boss. You got me.

FISBY

(*Smiles*)

Thanks . . . do you know the road?

SAKINI

No road, boss—just path for wagon cart and goat.

FISBY

Will a jeep make it?

SAKINI

We find out, boss.

31

FISBY

Naturally. How long will it take us?

SAKINI

Oh—not know until we arrive, boss.

FISBY

Naturally. Well, we might as well get started. I'll drive and you give directions.

SAKINI

Oh, very happy to go home.

FISBY

Where is the jeep?

SAKINI

Right here, boss.
(*He turns and claps his hands. The panels go up. The laundry line has been removed and the jeep pulled down center. The jeep is piled with Fisby's belongings. Perched high on the top of this pyramid sits a very old and very wrinkled* NATIVE WOMAN. SAKINI *pays no attention to her as he goes around the jeep test-kicking the tires. And the* OLD WOMAN *sits disinterested and aloof from what goes on below her.*)

FISBY

Hey, wait a minute! What's she doing up there?
(*He points to her. The* OLD WOMAN *sits with hands folded serenely, looking straight ahead.*)

SAKINI

She nice old lady hear we go to Tobiki village. She think she go along to visit grandson.

FISBY

Oh, she does. Well, you explain that I'm very sorry but she'll have to take a bus.

SAKINI

No buses to Tobiki. People very poor—can only travel on generosity.

FISBY

I'm sorry, but it's against regulations.

SAKINI

She not fall off, boss. She tied on.

FISBY

Well, untie her and get her down. She'll just have to find some other way to visit her grandson.

SAKINI

Her grandson mayor of Tobiki village. You make him lose face if you kick old grandmother off jeep.

FISBY

She's the mayor's grandmother?

SAKINI

Oh yes, boss.

FISBY

Well, since she's already tied on, I guess we can take her.
    (*He looks at the bundles.*)
Are all those *mine?*

SAKINI

Oh, no. Most of bundles belong to old lady. She think she visit three or four months so she bring own bed and cooking pots.

33

FISBY

Well, tell her to yell out if she sees any low branches coming.
            (*He starts to get in.*)
Let's get started.

SAKINI

Oh, can't go yet, boss.

FISBY

Why not?

SAKINI

Old lady's daughter not here.

FISBY

            (*Glances at watch*)
We can't wait for a lot of good-byes, Sakini!

SAKINI

            (*Looking behind* FISBY)
Oh, she come now—right on dot you bet.
            (CAPTAIN FISBY *turns to witness a squat young* NATIVE
            WOMAN *come on pushing a wheelbarrow loaded with
            bundles. She stops long enough to bow low to* FISBY—
            then begins to tie bundles onto the jeep.)

FISBY

Sakini, can't the old lady leave some of that stuff behind?

SAKINI

Not her things, boss. Belong to daughter.

FISBY

Wait a minute. Is the daughter planning on going with us, too?

SAKINI

Old lady very old. Who take care of her on trip?

34

FISBY

Well, I—

(THE DAUGHTER *takes the wheelbarrow and hurries off.*)
Hey—you come back! Sakini—tell her to come back. We can't carry any more bundles.

SAKINI

(*Calmly*)
Oh, she not go to get bundles, boss. She go to get children.

FISBY

Come here, Sakini. Now look—this sort of thing is always happening to me and I have to put a stop to it some place. This time I'm determined to succeed. It's not that I don't *want* to take them. But you can see for yourself, *there's no room left for kids!*

SAKINI

But daughter not go without children and old lady not go without daughter. And if old lady not go, mayor of Tobiki be mad at you.
(*Turns to see the DAUGHTER hurry back with three children in tow. They all bow politely to FISBY. Their mother then piles them on the hood of the jeep.*)

FISBY

For Pete's sake, Sakini, how does she expect me to see how to drive!

SAKINI

Old lady got very good eyesight. She sit on top and tell us when to turn.
(*At this point one of the CHILDREN climbs off the hood and points offstage.*)

CHILD
  A! Wasureta!

DAUGHTER
  Wasureta? Nanisa?

CHILD
  Fija dayo.
        (*The* CHILD *dashes offstage.*)

FISBY
  Now, where's *he* going?

SAKINI
        (*To* DAUGHTER)
  Doshtano?

DAUGHTER
  Fija turete kurendes!

SAKINI
        (*To* FISBY)
  He go to get goat.

FISBY
  A goat!

SAKINI
  Can't go and leave poor goat behind.

DAUGHTER
        (*Waves gaily to the* OLD WOMAN *on top of the jeep*)
  Okasan daijobu!
        (*She climbs the pyramid of bundles to settle beside her.*)

NOTE: The Luchuan dialect used throughout the play is merely a phonetic approximation.

36

FISBY

Well, right here is where we start seeing who's going to lose face. No goat is going to travel on this jeep.

SAKINI

You not like goats, boss?

FISBY

It has nothing to do with whether I like goats or not. I'm positive the colonel wouldn't like it.

SAKINI

But children not go without goat, mother not go without children, old lady not go without daughter—

FISBY

(*Repeats with* SAKINI)
—and if old lady not go, the mayor of Tobiki be mad at you!
(FISBY *sees the goat being led on by the* SMALL BOY.)
Oh, no!

SAKINI

Everybody here, boss. Goat not got children. Goat unmarried lady goat.

FISBY

All right, all right. Put it on the hood with the kids.
(*The goat is placed on the hood and held by the* CHIL-DREN.)
We've got to get started or we'll never get off the ground.

SAKINI

All ready to go, boss. You get in now. Nobody else going.
(*But before* FISBY *can climb in an* OLD MAN *comes hurry-ing in and, without looking to the right or left, climbs on the back of the jeep and settles down.*)

37

FISBY
 Now who the hell is he?

SAKINI
 (*Looks at* OLD MAN)
 Now who the hell is he?
 (*Back to* FISBY)
 Not know, boss, never see before.

FISBY
 Is he a relation of theirs?

SAKINI
 (*To the woman on top of the jeep*)
 Kore dare?

MOTHER
 Mitakoto nai hito desu.

SAKINI
 She say she never see him before, boss.

FISBY
 Well, ask him what he's doing here!

SAKINI
 (*Goes to the* OLD MAN)
 Ojisan, doshtano?

OLD MAN
 Washimo notte ikuyo.

SAKINI
 He say he see people going somewhere on trip and he think maybe he like to go somewhere, too.

38

FISBY

Tell him to get off and get off quick!

SAKINI

Dame dayo, ojisan, orina, orina!

OLD MAN

(*Angrily*)

Fija noserunnera washimo noruyo!

SAKINI

He say why not take him? You take goat. He say maybe you think he not as good as goat?

FISBY

Look, Sakini, explain to him that the eyes of the world are on Washington and the eyes of Washington are on me. I can't be responsible for—

(*But before this can be translated,* COLONEL PURDY *stalks on and comes to an abrupt halt.*)

PURDY

Captain Fisby!

FISBY

Yes, sir.

PURDY

What in the name of Occupation do you think you're doing!

FISBY

It's hard to explain, sir. . . . I, ah . . . ah . . .

(*As he founders, the* OLD LADY *on top of the bundles comes to life. She looks down and screams shrilly.*)

39

OLD LADY

Yakamashii oyajijana, hayo *iko, iko!*

PURDY

What is *she* saying?

SAKINI

She say . . . tell fat old man to shut up so we can get started!
(*As* COLONEL PURDY'S *jaw drops, the panels drop also.*)

BLACKOUT

Scene 3

SCENE: Tobiki village.

TIME: Ten days later.

AT RISE: All the bamboo panels are down. SAKINI walks in
           front of them to the center of the stage from the
           wings.

SAKINI
> (Bows)

Distance from Headquarters to Tobiki village by map . . . two
  inches.
By horse . . . three days.
By foot . . . four days.
By jeep . . . ten days.
Explanation:
Captain want to go to Tobiki.
Children want to go ocean. Never see ocean.
We see ocean.
Captain want to go to Tobiki.
Old lady's daughter want to visit Awasi.
We go Awasi.
Old lady make second mistake.
Captain demand we go Tobiki.
Ancient man have cousin in Yatoda.
We go Yatoda.
Damn fool old lady not know one road from another.
Now we arrive Tobiki.

Tobiki welcome rice and democracy.

(*He claps his hands for the panels to be raised, then walks into the scene. The destitute village of Tobiki is revealed with its sagging huts and its ragged villagers grouped in the square just outside of Captain Fisby's office. This is a small bamboo structure with a thatched roof. It has a makeshift desk and field telephone. There is a cot crowded against the upper wall.* FISBY, *his glasses on, sits studying Plan B. He puts the document down, and, taking off his glasses, calls to* SAKINI.)

FISBY

Sakini!

SAKINI

Right here, boss. Not asleep, boss.

FISBY

Good. According to Plan B, my first job here is to hold a public meeting.

SAKINI

Public waiting in public square ... eager to meet new boss, boss.

FISBY

Good. Now, Plan B calls for a lecture on the ABC's of democracy.

(*He turns to* SAKINI.)

Make sure they understand that I come as a friend of the people. That we intend to lift the yoke of oppression from their shoulders.

SAKINI

Oh, they like that, boss. This their favorite speech.

42

FISBY

What do you mean, their favorite speech?

SAKINI

Oh, Japanese say same things when they come, boss. Then take everything.

FISBY

Well, we're not here to *take* anything.

SAKINI

They got nothing left to take away, boss.

FISBY

(*Annoyed*)
Well, if they *did* have, we wouldn't take it. We're here to *give* them something.

SAKINI

Oh, not get angry, boss. We not mind. After eight centuries we get used to it. When friends come now, we hide things quick as the dickens.

FISBY

(*Rises, a little upset*)
Well, I guess it's up to me to convince them we really are friends. Let's meet the villagers.
(*He picks up his papers.*)
And let them meet Plan B.
(*As they step out the door to the office, the villagers rise and bow respectfully in unison.* FISBY *surveys them.*)

SAKINI

(*Introducing* FISBY)
Amerikano Taisho-san, Captain Fisby.

FISBY

> (*Bows in return*)

Well, we might as well get started, Sakini.

> (*He finds a box and stands on it. He glances into Plan B and clears his throat.*)

Citizens of Tobiki village. I—

SAKINI

> (*Interrupts him*)

Sorry, boss. Can't begin lecture yet.

FISBY

Why not?

SAKINI

Not good manners. People bring you gifts. You must accept gifts first.

FISBY

But I'm here to bring gifts from my government to them.

SAKINI

Very rude to make people feel poor, boss.

FISBY

I don't want to make anyone feel poor, but—

SAKINI

You make them lose face if you refuse, boss. They not accept democracy from you.

FISBY

All right. All right, then. Say to them that I'll accept their gifts in the name of the United States Occupation Forces.

SAKINI
> (*Turns to the* VILLAGERS)

Soreja moratte okuyo!
> (MR. HOKAIDA, *an enormous villager in tattered peasant clothes, steps forward.*)

MR. HOKAIDA
> (*Bows diffidently and offers his present to* FISBY)

Amerika-san, korewo dozo.

SAKINI
This Mr. Hokaida, boss. He give you fine present.

FISBY
Thank you. Thank you very much.
> (*He takes it and turns to* SAKINI *puzzled.*)

What is it?

SAKINI
You not know?

FISBY
No.

SAKINI
Oh, where you been all your life, boss?

FISBY
Living without one of these, I guess.

SAKINI
Is very splendid cricket cage, boss.

FISBY
What's it used for?

45

SAKINI

Keep cricket in.

FISBY

Why?

SAKINI

So Fortune smile on you. Cricket very good luck.

FISBY

But there's no cricket in it.

SAKINI

Bad luck to give cricket. You must catch your own fortune.
No one can get it for you.

FISBY

(*Considers this*)
Thank him and tell him I'll keep my eye out for a cricket.

SAKINI

Ya, arigato.
(MR. HOKAIDA *bows away as an* ANCIENT NATIVE *steps forward and bows.*)
This Mr. Omura. He bring you gift of chopsticks.

MR. OMURA

Korede mainichi gochiso wo, dozo.

SAKINI

He say: May only food of gods touch your lips.
(*As* FISBY *bows,* MR. SUMATA, *a nervous citizen in a torn straw hat, pushes his way toward* SAKINI.)

MR. SUMATA

Sugu modotte kuruyo!

SAKINI
  Doshtandes?

MR. SUMATA
  Ima sugu presento motte kuruyo.
          (*He turns and runs hurriedly off stage right.*)

FISBY
  What was that?

SAKINI
  That Mr. Sumata. He have present at home for you. He say not
  go away until he get.
          (*A rather handsome young Tobikian,* MR. SEIKO, *now
          steps forward and extends a pair of wooden sandals.*)

MR. SEIKO
  Dozo korewo chakini.

SAKINI
  This Mr. Seiko. He brings you geta.

FISBY
  Geta?

SAKINI
  Wooden sandals. Very comfortable for tired feet. He say: May
  you walk in prosperity.

FISBY
  Tell him I shall walk in the—the cool—meadow—of—of pleasant
  memories. Is that all right?

SAKINI
  Oh, that's very pretty, boss.
          (*He turns to* MR. SEIKO.)
  Ya, arigato, Seiko-san.

MR. SEIKO
>*(Beams, bows, and backs away)*

Iya, kosi no itari desu.

SAKINI

He say you do him honor.
>*(Here a chunky, flat-faced, aggressive* YOUNG WOMAN
>*with heavy glasses pushes forward with her present.)*

Oh, this Miss Higa Jiga—unmarried lady. She bring you three eggs.

FISBY

Tell her I shall eat them for breakfast.
>*(He bows to her.)*

SAKINI

Captain-san, daisuki desu.

MISS HIGA JIGA

Kame no tamago desu.
>*(She bows away.)*

SAKINI

She say she hope you enjoy turtle eggs.

FISBY
>*(Grins and bows to her)*

She'll never know.

SAKINI

You very big success. They sure like you already.
>*(Another* VILLAGER *steps forward and offers a gift.)*

This Mr. Keora. He bring you another cricket cage. Minus cricket.

FISBY

Say to him—that my prospects of good fortune are doubled.
(*He looks rather pleased with himself.*)

SAKINI

Kagowa futatsu de, un wa bai!

MR. KEORA

Hoho! Naka naka shiteki desna!
(*He bows away.*)

SAKINI

He say you are inspired poet.

FISBY

(*Modestly*)
It's all in getting the hang of it.

SAKINI

(*Introducing the next citizen, a very* OLD MAN *leaning on
a stick*)
This old man Mr. Oshira. He bring you fine lacquered cup he
make himself.

FISBY

Tell him I'm forever in his debt for such a beautiful gift.

OSHIRA

You are most welcome, Captain.

FISBY

(*Turns to him in surprise*)
You speak English!

49

SAKINI

Mr. Oshira teach me English when I am little boy in Tobiki.

OSHIRA

In my youth I work in Manila. How is Mr. McKinley?

FISBY

(*Puzzled for a moment*)
Who? Oh—President McKinley. I'm afraid someone shot him.

OSHIRA

I am sad.

FISBY

It was a long time ago.

OSHIRA

Yes, a long time.
(*He indicates the cup.*)
May August moon fill your cup.

FISBY

May I ask, why an August moon?

OSHIRA

All moons good, but August moon little older, little wiser.

FISBY

Did Sakini say you made this cup yourself?

OSHIRA

Oh, yes. I learned from my father before me who learned from his father before him. Is our heritage.

50

SAKINI

Look, boss, this cup thin as paper, carved from one block of wood. Then painted many times with red lacquer.

FISBY

And did you paint the gold fish inside?

OSHIRA

(*Nods*)
It is imperfect.

SAKINI

When Mr. Oshira little boy, he work ten years to learn how to paint gold fish exactly like his papa paint.

FISBY

It's just beautiful! Can you still make things like this?

OSHIRA

One does not forget.

FISBY

Sakini, here's an industry we can start right away. This is a lost art.
(*Turns to* OSHIRA)
Is there any way we could mass-produce these?

OSHIRA

Mass-produce?

FISBY

You know—set up machines and turn them out by the gross.

OSHIRA

    (*Shakes his head*)

I take pride in making one cup at time, Captain. How can I take pride in work of machine?

FISBY

How many of these could you turn out in a day?

OSHIRA

If I work hard, maybe one or two a week.

FISBY

    (*Disappointed*)

Well, it's a start. Make as many as you can. We'll send them up to the American Post Exchange and sell them as fast as you can turn them out.

OSHIRA

I shall do my best. The swiftness of my youth has deserted me, sir.

    (*He bows and moves back.*)

But I shall make fewer mistakes.

FISBY

    (*Excitedly*)

Sakini, tell Mr. Omura to make up a batch of chopsticks. Have everybody get to work making cricket cages, wooden sandals and—

    (*Pointing*)

—these straw hats. We'll put this village in the souvenir business.

SAKINI

We all make money, boss?

FISBY

If they can turn out enough of these things, I guarantee the recovery of Tobiki village. Tell them.

SAKINI

Kore dondon tskuru yoni...
> (*There is a general exchange of chatter and approval.*)
They say they make everything, fast as the dickens, boss.

FISBY

Good. We're in business. Now ask them if they'd mind postponing the rest of the gifts until later. I'd like to tell them what *we're* planning for *them*.

SAKINI

Sa, sono hanashi shiyo.

CITIZENS

No agerumono naiyo! Hanashi wo kiko.

SAKINI

They say sure. They got no more presents anyhow.

FISBY

Good. First I want to tell them about the school we're going to build for their children. All set to translate?

SAKINI

All set.

FISBY

All right.
> (*He consults Plan B.*)
Plan B says the direct approach is most effective. This is it.
> (*He steps back up on a box and looks forcefully at his listeners. Then he points a dramatic finger at them.*)
Do you want to be ignorant?

53

SAKINI

    (Also points a finger)

Issho bakaja dame daro?

    (The CITIZENS *make a noise that sounds like "Hai.")*

FISBY

What did they say?

SAKINI

They say "Yes."

FISBY

What do you mean, "yes"? They *want* to be ignorant?

SAKINI

No, boss. But in Luchuan "yes" means "no." They say "yes," they *not* want to be ignorant.

FISBY

Oh.

    (He turns back to his rapt audience and assumes his forensic posture.)

Do you want your *children* to be ignorant?

SAKINI

Issho kodomotachi mo bakaja dame daro?

    (The VILLAGERS *respond quickly with a noise that sounds like "Iie")*

FISBY

What did they say then?

SAKINI

They say "No."

FISBY

"No" they do, or "No" they don't?

SAKINI

Yes, they not want no ignorant children.

FISBY

Good.
> (*He turns back to the* VILLAGERS.)

Then this is what my government is planning to do for you.
First there will be daily issues of rice for everyone.

SAKINI

Mazu kome no hykyu!
> (*The* VILLAGERS *cheer.*)

FISBY

We will build a fine new school here for your children.
> (*Then recalling Colonel Purdy's dictum*)

Pentagon-shaped.

SAKINI

Gakko taterundayo katachi wa—
> (*He flounders.*)

Ah—Pentagon.
> (*The* CITIZENS *look at each other, puzzled.*)

MISS HIGA JIGA

Nandesutte?

SAKINI

Pentagon.

MISS HIGA JIGA

Sore wa nandesuka?

SAKINI

They say what is Pentagon? Never hear before.

FISBY

Never heard of the *Pentagon!*

SAKINI

No, boss.

FISBY

Well, they certainly do need a school here. The Pentagon is—
is—
(*He looks down at their eager faces.*)
Well, it really means five-sided.

SAKINI

Kabega itsutsusa, ii, ni, san, yon, go.
(*Holds up five fingers. There is a burst of laughter from
the* CITIZENS.)

MISS HIGA JIGA
(*Giggling*)
Ara, gokakuno kodomo nante arimasenyo.

SAKINI

They say no children in Tobiki got five sides.

FISBY

The *school* will be five-sided—like a building in Washington.

SAKINI

(*Explains*)
Chigauyo, chigauyo, onaji mono arundes yo, Washington ni.
(*There is a decided reaction of approval.* SAKINI *turns
back to* FISBY.)
They very impressed.

56

FISBY
> (*Continuing*)
Everyone will learn about democracy.

SAKINI
> Mazu minshu shugi bera-bera bera-bera.

MISS HIGA JIGA
> Minshu shugi bera-bera bera-bera?

SAKINI
> They say: Explain what is democracy. They know what rice is.

FISBY
> Oh.
> (*He scratches his head.*)
> Well, it's a system of self-determination. It's—it's the right to make the wrong choice.

SAKINI
> Machigattemo iindayo.
> (*They look up blankly, silently.*)

FISBY
> I don't think we're getting the point over. Explain that if I don't like the way Uncle Sam treats me, I can write the President himself and tell him so.

SAKINI
> Daitoryo ni tegami kaitemo iinosa.
> (*The* VILLAGERS *all laugh heartily.*)

MISS HIGA JIGA
> Masaka soonakoto!

57

SAKINI

>*(Triumphantly)*
They say: But do you *send* the letters?

FISBY

Let's get on with the lecture.
>*(He turns back to the citizens and reads from Plan B.)*
Tell them hereafter all men will be free and equal. . . .

SAKINI

Subete, jiyuu, to byodo, de ar, de ar.

FISBY

>*(Increases his tempo and volume)*
Without discrimination . . .

SAKINI

>*(Taking* FISBY's *tone)*
Sabetsu taigoo haishi de ar.

FISBY

The will of the majority will rule!

SAKINI

Subete minna de kime, de ar!

FISBY

>*(Finishing with a flourish)*
And Tobiki village will take its place in the brotherhood of democratic peoples the world over!

SAKINI

>*(Rising to new demagogic heights)*
Koshite, Tobiki, jiyuu, Okinawa, byodo sabetsu, taigu—haishi, jiyuu, byodo de ar, de ar.
>*(A great burst of applause greets Sakini's performance.*
>*He turns to* FISBY.)
We going over big, boss.

FISBY

    (Agrees with a nod)
Now to get this village organized. Is the mayor here?

SAKINI

    (Points)
Mr. Omura is mayor, boss.
    (MR. OMURA *steps forward.*)
He only one in Tobiki with white coat.

FISBY

    (Glances at the worn, ragged coat)
It looks to me as if you'll have to get a new coat or a new mayor soon.

SAKINI

Better keep mayor, boss. Impossible to get white coat.

FISBY

Well, since we've got a mayor, we only have to find a Chief of Agriculture and a Chief of Police. That's going to present a problem.

SAKINI

No problem, boss. You just look over gifts and see who give you best gift. Then you give him best job.

FISBY

Sakini, that is *not* the democratic way. The people themselves must choose the man best qualified. Tell them they are to elect their own Chief of Agriculture.

SAKINI

Sah! Senkyo desu. Mazu Chief of Agriculture.

WOMEN VILLAGERS
>(*Push* MR. SIEKO *forward shouting*)
>Seiko-san, Seiko-san ga ii, Seiko-san!

SAKINI

They say they elect Mr. Seiko. He best qualified for agriculture.

FISBY

He's an experienced farmer?

SAKINI

No, boss. He's artist. He draw lovely picture of golden wheat stalk with pretty green butterfly.

FISBY

Drawing pictures of wheat doesn't make him a wheat expert.

SAKINI

Wheat not grow here anyhow, boss. Only sweet potatoes.

FISBY

All right, all right! If he's their choice.

SEIKO

Ano! Watashimo shiroi koto wo.

SAKINI

He say do he get white coat like the mayor?

FISBY

Tell him I'll get him a helmet that says "Chief of Agriculture" on it.

SAKINI

Yoshi, yoshi, kammuri ageruyo.
>(SEIKO *bows and backs away*.)

FISBY

Next we want to elect a Chief of Police.

SAKINI

Kondowa Chief of Police!

VILLAGERS

(*Clamor and push the fat* MR. HOKAIDA *forward*)
Hokaida-san. Soda, soda. Hokaida-san.

FISBY

What are *his* qualifications for office?

SAKINI

People afraid of him. He champion wrestler.
(MR. HOKAIDA *flexes his muscles.*)

FISBY

Well, no one can say this isn't self-determination.

MR. HOKAIDA

Washime ano kammuri wo.

SAKINI

He say do he get helmet too?

FISBY

(*Nods*)
I'll requisition another helmet.

SAKINI

Agemasuyo.

MR. HOKAIDA

(*Bows smiling*)
Ya, doomo.

FISBY

Now for the ladies. We intend to organize a Ladies' League for Democratic Action. We'll want to elect a League President.

SAKINI

Oh, ladies never vote before—they like that.
(*He turns to the* LADIES.)
Kondowa Ladies' League for Democratic Action!
(*This announcement is greeted by excited chatter. The* LADIES *push* MISS HIGA JIGA *forward.*)

LADIES

Higa-Jiga-san—Higa-Jiga-san!

SAKINI

They say they elect Miss Higa Jiga. They think she make classy president.

MISS HIGA JIGA
(*Points to her head*)
Ano, watashi nimo ano booshio . . .

FISBY

(*Laughs*)
All right, I'll see that she gets a helmet, too. Now ask them if they have any question they'd like to ask *me*.

SAKINI

Sa, nanka kikitai koto ga attara.

OLD WOMAN
Sakini-san, ima nanji kaina?

SAKINI

They say they like to know what time is it?

62

FISBY
          (*Puzzled*)
     Time?
          (*Glances at his watch*)
     Quarter of five, why?

SAKINI
     They say they got to hurry then. They not like to miss sunset.
     This is time of day they sit in pine grove, sip tea and watch sun
     go down.

FISBY
     All right, thank them and tell them they can go have tea in the
     pine grove.

SAKINI
     Ya, minna kaette mo iiyo.
          (*They bow and, chattering happily among themselves,
          go off right.* FISBY *gathers up his gifts.*)

FISBY
     How do you think we did, Sakini?

SAKINI
     They cooperate, boss. Future look very rosy.

FISBY
     Where do you think I can find a cricket?

SAKINI
     One come along. May have one in house now and not know it.

FISBY
     Well, I'll take these things in and get started on my Progress
     Report.
          (*He goes to the office hut.*)

SAKINI

   I take a little snooze then. Public speaking very exhausting.

FISBY

>   (*As he goes inside*)
>   *I* think I handled it pretty well.⏋
>
>> (*He sits down at his desk. He examines his gifts and then,
>> putting on his glasses, begins to study Plan B again. After
>> a moment,* MR. SUMATA *enters from the right. He carries
>> a couple of battered suitcases. He is followed by* LOTUS
>> BLOSSOM, *a petite and lovely geisha girl in traditional cos-
>> tume. When they are about center stage, young* MR.
>> SEIKO *runs up after the geisha girl. She turns to him.*)

SEIKO

   Ano, chotto ...

LOTUS BLOSSOM

   Ara! Nani?

SUMATA

>   (*Steps in front of* SEIKO *and points an angry finger under
>   his nose*)
>   Dame, dame, atchi ike.
>   (SEIKO *bows head and retreats.* MR. SUMATA *then turns to*
>   SAKINI.)
>   Amerika-san doko?

SAKINI

>   (*Indicates the office*)
>   Asco.

SUMATA

>   (*Indicates geisha girl*)
>   Kore tsurete kitandayo.

SAKINI
Oh? Do-sunno?

SUMATA
Kore Taisho-san ni agetainja.
(*He bows and goes off quickly, almost running. The* GEISHA *remains with* SAKINI. SAKINI *smiles and steps inside the office. He stands behind* FISBY.)

SAKINI
You busy, boss?

FISBY
(*Without turning around to him*)
Yes, but what is it?

SAKINI
Mr. Sumata leave present for you, boss.

FISBY
Put it on the shelf where it'll be out of the way.

SAKINI
(*Glances back outside*)
Not able to do, boss. Present get mad.

FISBY
(*Turns around*)
What's this about, Sakini?

SAKINI
(*Motions to the* GEISHA, *who steps inside smiling. She bows.*)
Here you are, boss.

65

FISBY
> (*Rising*)

Who is *she?*

SAKINI

Souvenir.

FISBY

What are you talking about?

SAKINI

Present from Mr. Sumata.

FISBY

Wait a minute. Is he kidding? I can't accept a human present.

SAKINI

Oh, human present very lovely. Introducing Lotus Blossom, geisha girl first class.
> (*He turns to* LOTUS BLOSSOM)

Amerika-san no Captain Fisby.

LOTUS BLOSSOM
> (*Smiling happily*)

Ara, ii otokomaene! Watashi sukidawa.

SAKINI

She say she very happy to belong to handsome captain. She say she serve you well.

FISBY

She's not going to serve me at all. You get that Mr. Sumata and tell him I'm returning his present.

66

SAKINI

Impossible to do, boss. Mr. Sumata leave present and go up
mountains to visit cousin. He say good-bye and wish you much
success in Tobiki.

LOTUS BLOSSOM

(*Sweetly*)

Watashi kokoni sumun desho?

SAKINI

She say, where do you want her to stay, boss?

FISBY

You tell her I don't care where she stays. She can't stay here.

SAKINI

(*Shocked*)

Where she go then? She got no home. Mr. Sumata already gone
away.

FISBY

Well, find her a place for the time being.

SAKINI

(*Grins*)

Plenty of room in my house, boss. Just me and my grandpapa.

FISBY

No, I can't do that. Sit her over on that box until I can think
where to put her.

SAKINI

You can put her in business, boss.

67

FISBY

You keep a civil tongue in your head, Sakini.

LOTUS BLOSSOM

(*Comes over to* FISBY, *whom she has been watching with great interest*)

Okimono to ozohri motte kimasune.

SAKINI

She like to put on your sandals and kimono for you. She trained to please you, boss.

FISBY

I know what she's trained to do. And I don't need any translation.

(*He sits down at his desk again.*)

Sakini ... take my supplies out of the shack and bring them over here. We'll set her up there where I can keep an eye on her.

SAKINI

Not very democratic, boss. You make her lose face if she not make you comfortable, boss. She think she bad geisha girl.

FISBY

You tell her ... I've got some face to save, too ... so she can just forget this Oriental hanky-panky.

SAKINI

Anta irantesa!

LOTUS BLOSSOM

(*Waves him away*)

Ara, nani ittennoyo. Imasara ikettatte ikarenai desho.

FISBY

Well, what did she say?

68

SAKINI

She say for me to go on home to grandpapa ... she first-class geisha girl ... she know her business. Good night, boss.

(FISBY stands eyeing LOTUS BLOSSOM as SAKINI goes out. The lights go down quickly. During the brief blackout, the two center panels are lowered, shutting out the village street. The office of Colonel Purdy is swung into place in the last panel right. The lights come up on PURDY twisting the bell on his field telephone.)

PURDY

What do you mean ... there's no answer? Well, keep trying. I'm not the kind of a man to take "no answer" for an answer.

(The lights come up on the opposite side of the stage in Fisby's office. FISBY is holding onto his jacket buttons. LOTUS BLOSSOM stands in front of him holding out his robe. She is gently persistent and puzzled at his reticence.)

FISBY

It's *not* a kimono ... it's a bathrobe. And I don't *want* to put it on.

LOTUS BLOSSOM

(Reaches to unbutton his jacket)
Sa! Shizukani shimasho ne.

FISBY

No, it's against regulations.

(Phone rings. He takes the robe away from LOTUS BLOSSOM and sits on it. Then he picks up the phone.)
Hello!

PURDY

(Jumps)
You don't have to shout. I can hear you. This is Colonel Purdy.

69

FISBY

> (*Leaps to his feet and pushes* LOTUS BLOSSOM *behind him as if to hide her*)

Yes, sir.

PURDY

Just thought I'd check up on you. How are things going?
> (LOTUS BLOSSOM *begins to fan her master.*)

FISBY

Well, everything seems to be under control at the moment.
> (*He sits down and takes out a cigarette.* LOTUS BLOSSOM *promptly lights it for him.*)

PURDY

Anything *I* can do for you?

FISBY

> (*Pauses*)

I can't think of anything, sir.

PURDY

I realize it's bound to get lonely for you down there ... so you know what I'm going to do, my boy?

FISBY

> (LOTUS BLOSSOM *gets the geta and kneels before him.* FISBY *watches her apprehensively and asks* ...)

What are you going to do?

PURDY

I'll tell you. I'm going to send you some of my old *Adventure Magazines*.

70

FISBY

> (*As* LOTUS BLOSSOM *starts to take off his shoes*)

No, *no*. I don't want them.

> (*Into the phone*)

I mean . . . yes . . . thank you.

> (*He rises and twists about trying to pull his foot away
> from* LOTUS BLOSSOM.)

I'd like something to read.

PURDY

How are you getting along with the natives?

FISBY

> (*His leg over the chair.*)

The problem here, sir, is a very old one. It seems to be a question of who's going to lose face.

PURDY

I understand. As Mrs. Purdy says, "East is East and West is West, and there can be no Twain." But you're making progress?

FISBY

Nothing I'd like to put on paper, sir.

> (LOTUS BLOSSOM *gets his shoes off and slips the sandals
> on.*)

PURDY

Well, when things get moving down there, send in a detailed Progress Report.

FISBY

If that's what you want, sir.

> (LOTUS BLOSSOM *recovers the robe. She reaches out to
> unbutton his jacket.*)

71

PURDY

You'll find these people lack the capacity for sustained endeavor. Don't hesitate to build a fire under them.

FISBY

(*Struggling to keep his jacket on*)
That won't be necessary, sir.

PURDY

Don't forget ... the eyes of Washington are on you, Fisby.

FISBY

(*As* LOTUS BLOSSOM *tries to pull his jacket over his head*)
I hope not, sir.

PURDY

(*Ponders*)
Fisby, it just occurred to me. Have you given any thought to physical education?

FISBY

If I may say so, sir ...
(LOTUS BLOSSOM *gets one arm out*)
I consider the suggestion ...
(*He hugs the other sleeve*)
a masterpiece of timeliness.
(*He gets down on one knee.*)

PURDY

Thank you, my boy.
(*Pauses*)
Could you use a deck of cards?
Hello? Hello, Fisby ... you're getting weak.
(*As* FISBY *looks back at the telephone and nods in complete agreement, the two scenes black out simultane-*

ously. The panels fall. A spot picks up SAKINI *as he steps from the wings.*)

SAKINI
Discreet place to stop now and sip soothing cup of jasmine tea.
Conclusion?
Not yet.
Continuation shortly.
Lotus Blossom not lose face!
(*He bows.*)

THE CURTAIN FALLS

ACT TWO

Scene I

SCENE: *Tobiki village.*

TIME: *A few days later.*

AT RISE: *All the panels are down.* SAKINI *enters from the wings and crosses down to the footlights center. He bows to the audience.*

SAKINI
Lovely ladies, kind gentlemen:
Most traveled person in history of world is summer sun.
Each day must visit each man no matter where he live on globe.
Always welcome visitor.
Not bring gossip.
Not stay too long.
Not depart leaving bad taste of rude comment.
But summer sun never tell topside of world what bottomside like.
So bottomside must speak for self.
We continue with little story of Tobiki.
Center of industry.
Seat of democracy.
        (*He beams.*)
Home of geisha girl.
        (*He goes to the right proscenium arch as all the panels are raised, revealing the empty street outside of Fisby's office.* FISBY *enters, starts across stage,* SAKINI *falling in step behind him.*)
Was wondering what happened to you, boss?

FISBY

>   *(Stops)*
>   I went down to inspect the sweet-potato fields. Sakini, no one was there. The potatoes were piled up, but no one was working.

SAKINI

>   Very hot day, boss.

FISBY

>   But I can't find my Chief of Agriculture. Or the Mayor, or the Chief of Police. Where is everybody?

SAKINI

>   Lotus Blossom leave belongings over at Awasi—got no way to bring things here. So—everybody take wheelbarrow to help move Lotus Blossom to Tobiki.

FISBY

>   And has she got so many things that it takes my entire staff to move her to this village?

SAKINI

>   No, boss, but Chief of Police not trust Chief of Agriculture, and Mayor not trust Mr. Oshira, so all go.

FISBY

>   Mr. Oshira? That old man!

SAKINI

>   He's old, boss, but not dead.

FISBY

>   A fine way for officials to behave! You tell them I want to see them the moment they come back.
>   *(He starts for his office.)*
>   A fine thing!

SAKINI

Nothing to worry about, boss. They not beat your time. You own Lotus Blossom.

FISBY

I do *not* own her. It's not a question of—of—
(*He sits down at his desk.*)
Well, this sort of nonsense isn't going to stop my work.
(*He shifts the papers on his desk.*)
I intend to get started on that schoolhouse today. We've got the materials, so all we need now is some good carpenters.
(*He turns to* SAKINI, *who has followed him inside.*)
Who is the best carpenter in the village?

SAKINI

Mr. Sumata.

FISBY

Fine. Get hold of him. Wait a minute! Isn't he the joker who gave me Lotus Blossom?

SAKINI

Mr. Sumata has finger in lots of pies, boss.

FISBY

Well, since he's vanished, who is the next best carpenter?

SAKINI

Father of Mr. Sumata.

FISBY

Where is he?

SAKINI

Go on vacation with Mr. Sumata.

79

FISBY

> (*Beginning to get annoyed*)

Well, who is the *third* best carpenter then?

SAKINI

No more, boss. Only Sumata and son. They have what you call monopoly.

FISBY

There's something fishy about their disappearing.

> (MISS HIGA JIGA, *wearing a red helmet with flowers, followed by several other* LADIES, *comes storming across the stage to the office door.* SAKINI *hears them and goes to the door.*)

MISS HIGA JIGA

> (*Angrily*)

Watashitachi sabetsu taigu desyo!

FISBY

> (*Goes to the door also.*)

What's the matter with her?

SAKINI

Miss Higa Jiga say do you know what we got in this village, boss? Discrimination.

FISBY

> (*Wearily*)

Where?

> (SAKINI *turns to* MISS HIGA JIGA.)

MISS HIGA JIGA

> (*Indignantly*)

Watashitachi hykyu matte itara Lotus Blossom ga kite clarku

ga anata desuka ma dozo kochirae watashitachi nijikan mo machi mashita yo.

SAKINI

She say that Ladies' League for Democratic Action wait in line for rice rations. Along come Lotus Blossom and ration clerks say, "Oh, how do you do. Oh, please don't stand in line. You come inside and have cup of tea." Then clerks shut up warehouse and leave Ladies' League waiting in sun two hours.

FISBY

It's things like this that undermine the democratic ideal. You tell Miss Higa Jiga I intend to do something about it.
(*He storms into his office.*)

SAKINI

(*Turns to* MISS HIGA JIGA)
Nantoka shimasuyo.

FISBY

I can see right now we're going to have to get rid of the disrupting factor in our recovery.
(*He picks up the field telephone and twists the handle.*)
Get me Major McEvoy at Awasi.

SAKINI

(*Follows* FISBY *inside*)
What are you going to do, boss?

FISBY

This village isn't big enough for Plan B and a geisha girl.

SAKINI

Oh, boss, Tobiki never have geisha girl before. We like very much.

81

FISBY

> She has to go.
>> (*Then into the telephone*)
>
> Major McEvoy? Captain Fisby at Tobiki. I have a request from one of my people to transfer to your village. Yes, it's a female citizen. Profession? Well...
>> (*He looks at* SAKINI.)

SAKINI

> Oh, please not send her away, boss. Not democratic.

FISBY

> As a matter of fact her name *is* Lotus Blossom. *How* did *you* know? What do you mean, what am I trying to put over on you? Oh, you did?
>> (*He hangs up. Then he glares at* SAKINI.)

SAKINI

>> (*With great innocence*)
>
> He knows Lotus Blossom, boss?

FISBY

> Very well. She was at Awasi and damn near wrecked his whole plan for recovery. She's been booted out of every village by every commander on the island.

SAKINI

> Oh, poor little Lotus Blossom.

FISBY

> Poor little Lotus Blossom my eye. She upsets every village she's in.

SAKINI

> Not her fault she beautiful, boss.

FISBY

No wonder that Mr. Sumata disappeared. The major paid him a hundred yen to get her out of his village.

SAKINI

(*Eagerly*)

You keep her now, boss?

FISBY

I have to.

(*He points a finger at* SAKINI.)

Well, she's not going to get away with causing dissension in *my* village!

(MISS HIGA JIGA, *weary of waiting outside, storms in*)

MISS HIGA JIGA

Doshte itadakemasno Daitoryo ni tegami wo kakimasawayo.

FISBY

(*Pleads*)

Tell her to go away.

SAKINI

She say she waiting for some democratic action. She say if she don't get it, she thinks she write this Uncle Sam you talk about.

FISBY

Now, look. I don't want complaints going into Headquarters. Tell her discrimination is being eliminated.

SAKINI

Sabetsu yamemasyo.

MISS HIGA JIGA

Yamenakutemo iinoyo, watashitachi nimo wakete itadakeba.

83

SAKINI

Miss Higa Jiga say please not eliminate discrimination. She say just give her some too.

FISBY

And just what does she mean by that?

SAKINI

She say Lotus Blossom unfair competition.

FISBY

Granted.

SAKINI

She say you promise everybody going to be equal.

FISBY

I intend to keep my word.

SAKINI

Well, she say she can't be equal unless she has everything Lotus Blossom has.

FISBY

What Lotus Blossom's got, the Government doesn't issue.

SAKINI

(*Taking a piece of paper which* MISS HIGA JIGA *waves*)
She make list, boss. Shall I read, boss?

FISBY

Go ahead.

84

SAKINI

She wants you to get her and ladies in League following items:
A. Red stuff to put on lips like geisha.
B. Stuff that smell pretty—

FISBY

Now, *just* wait a minute. What would H.Q. think if I requisi-
tioned lipstick!

SAKINI

(*Hands list back to* MISS HIGA JIGA)
Dame desuyo.

MISS HIGA JIGA

Jaa Daitoryo ni tegami wo dashimaswa.

SAKINI

She say she sorry, but now she guess she just have to write
this letter to Uncle Samuel after all.

FISBY

(*Throws up his hands*)
All right. *All Right!* Tell her I'll call up the post exchange at
Awasi and see if they have any shaving powder and toilet
water.

SAKINI

Ya, katte agemasuyo.

MISS HIGA JIGA

(*Beams*)
Ano wasure naidene bobby pin.

SAKINI

She say, not forget bobby pins for hair.

FISBY

I think I might have been happier in the submarine command.

MISS HIGA JIGA

(Stops as she is about to go.)

Mohitotsu onegai watashitachi mo mina geisha ni.

SAKINI

She say one more thing. Can you get Lotus Blossom to teach Ladies' League all to be geisha girls?

FISBY

(Leaps to his feet)

Teach the innocent women of this village to be— *No!*

(MISS HIGA JIGA shrugs and goes outside. As FISBY sinks back at his desk, MISS HIGA JIGA talks excitedly to the WOMEN gathered outside. They run off giggling. FISBY sits at his desk and picks up Plan B.)

Plan B!

(He thumbs through its pages.)

Let's just see if Washington anticipated *this.*

(He buries his chin in his hands. SAKINI sits quietly watching him. Outside in the village street, LOTUS BLOSSOM enters and starts daintily toward the office. She has only gotten halfway when SEIKO overtakes her.)

SEIKO

(Panting)

Ano, chotto.

LOTUS BLOSSOM

(Stops and looks at him archly)

Nani?

SEIKO

>*(Takes a chrysanthemum bud from his waist)*
>
>Ano korewo dozo.

LOTUS BLOSSOM

>*(Takes it indifferently)*
>
>Ara, so arigato.

SEIKO

>*(Strikes his heart passionately)*
>
>Boku no, kono, hato, o.

LOTUS BLOSSOM

>*(Flicks her finger)*
>
>Anato no hahto? Ara shinzo ne.

SEIKO

>*(Disembowels himself with an imaginary knife)*
>
>Harakitte shinimas.

LOTUS BLOSSOM

>*(Yawns)*
>
>Imagoro sonnano hayaranai noyo.

SEIKO

>*(Points toward Fisby's office)*
>
>Soka Amerika-san ga iinoka?

LOTUS BLOSSOM

>*(Haughtily)*
>
>Nandeste! Sonnakoto yokeina osowa.

SEIKO

>*(Laughs decisively)*
>
>Nanda rashamon janaika.

87

LOTUS BLOSSOM

> (*Backs him up with an angry finger*)

Watashimo kotoni kansho shinaideyo.

SEIKO

> (*Bows his head*)

Gomen nasai iisugi deshta.

LOTUS BLOSSOM

> (*Points away*)

Atchi, itte.

> (SEIKO *sighs, turns and plods off toward the sweet-potato fields, crushed and dejected.* LOTUS BLOSSOM *tidies her hair and continues to the office. She calls in coyly*)

Fuisbee-san!

SAKINI

> (*Rises and looks out the door*)

Oh, what do you think, boss? Lotus Blossom back. She come to see you.

FISBY

And high time.

> (*He turns to face the door as* LOTUS BLOSSOM *enters and bows.*)

Where have *you* been all day? Never mind, I know—upsetting the agricultural horse cart.

LOTUS BLOSSOM

Fu-san no kao nikkori nasaruto totemo kawaii wa.

SAKINI

She say sun burst through the clouds now that you smile on her.

88

FISBY

I'm not smiling.
> (*She hands him Seiko's chrysanthemum bud.*)

SAKINI

Oh, boss, you know what she give you?

FISBY

The works.

SAKINI

When lady give gentleman chrysanthemum bud, in Okinawa
that means her heart is ready to unfold.

FISBY

Well, this is one bud that's not going to flower.

LOTUS BLOSSOM

> (*Offering a box she has brought*)
Kore otsukemono yo. Dozo.

SAKINI

She say, you like to eat some tsukemono? Tsukemono nice
thing to eat between meals.

FISBY

No.

LOTUS BLOSSOM

> (*Takes geta and kneels beside him*)
Dozo ohaki osobase.

FISBY

Tell her to *leave my feet* alone.

89

LOTUS BLOSSOM

    (*Studies* FISBY)

Kasa kaburu. Nisshabyo nanoyo.

SAKINI

She worried about you, boss. She say, when you go in hot sun, should wear *kasa*—that straw hat—on head.

FISBY

Tell her never mind about my feet or my head. I want her to stop interfering with the recovery program. To stop causing rebellion and making the men—ah—ah—discontented.

SAKINI

    (*Turns to* LOTUS BLOSSOM)

Jama shicha dame dayo.

LOTUS BLOSSOM

    (*Smiles*)

Fu-san ocha ikaga?

SAKINI

She say: You want some tea?

FISBY

    (*Throwing himself down on his cot*)

No.

LOTUS BLOSSOM

Shami demo hikimashoka?

SAKINI

She say: You want some music?

90

FISBY

No.

LOTUS BLOSSOM

    (*Giggles*)

Ara Fu-san-tara yaiteruno.

SAKINI

She say: You jealous, boss?

FISBY

    (*Mirthlessly*)

Ha!

LOTUS BLOSSOM

Honto ni doshita no?

SAKINI

She say: You want to tell her your troubles, boss?

FISBY

Why should I tell her my troubles?

SAKINI

She geisha girl, that's her *business*, boss.

FISBY

Some business.

LOTUS BLOSSOM

Shoga naiwane. Mah soshite irasshai yo.

SAKINI

She say she hear about lack of cooperation here. She feel very bad. She say she want to help because you best boss she ever had. You not make her work and you not take money from her.

FISBY

> (*Sits up on his cot*)

Did the other men who owned her . . . hire her out and then take money from her?

SAKINI

Oh, sure.

FISBY

Well, where I come from we have a name for men who—who—do *that* sort of thing.

SAKINI

You have geisha business in America, too?

FISBY

> (*Rises*)

No! Sakini, you give her to understand I have no intention of putting her to—to work.

SAKINI

Why not, boss? She pay all her dues to Geisha Guild. She member in good standing.

FISBY

You mean they've got a union for this sort of thing?

SAKINI

Geisha girl have to be protected, boss. Must keep up rates.

FISBY

This is the most immoral thing I've ever heard of. Haven't you people any sense of shame?

SAKINI

We bad not to be ashamed, boss?

FISBY

Obviously, there is a fundamental difference between us that can't be reconciled. I don't say that where I come from there's no such thing as prostitution. But, by God, we don't have unions, set rates and collect dues!

SAKINI

But geisha girl not prostitute, boss.

FISBY

At least we have the decency—
(*He stops*)
What do you mean, geisha girls aren't prostitutes? Everybody knows what they do.

SAKINI

Then everybody wrong, boss.

FISBY

Well, what do they get paid for, then?

SAKINI

Hard to explain fundamental difference. Poor man like to feel rich. Rich man like to feel wise. Sad man like to feel happy. All go to geisha house and tell troubles to geisha girl. She listen politely and say, "Oh, that's too bad." She very pretty. She make tea, she sing, she dance, and pretty soon troubles go away. Is not worth something, boss?

FISBY

And that's *all* they do?

SAKINI

Very ancient and honorable profession.

FISBY

Look, Sakini, I apologize. I guess I jumped the gun. And I'm glad you explained. It sort of puts a new light on things.
(*He turns to* LOTUS BLOSSOM *and grins.*)

LOTUS BLOSSOM

Ara, kyuni nikkorisite, mada okotteru no.

SAKINI

She say: Why are you smiling at her all of a sudden? You mad or something?

FISBY

Tell her that I'm a dope. That I have a coconut for a head.

SAKINI

No use, boss. She not believe.

FISBY

Then will you ask her if she'd be kind enough to give geisha lessons to the Ladies' League for Democratic Action?

SAKINI

Odori ya shami Ladies' League ni oshiete?

LOTUS BLOSSOM

Er iiwa, demo kumiaiaga kowaiwane.

SAKINI

She say Geisha Guild closed shop, but she teach if you not report her.
(*At this point the men of the village come across the square and stop before the office.* LOTUS BLOSSOM *goes to*

94

the door. Immediately there are ohs and ahs from the men.)

FISBY

What is that?

SAKINI

Sound like Okinawan wolf call, boss.

FISBY

Well, let's find out.
(*He goes outside to face the group, followed by* SAKINI.)
Ask what's the matter.

SAKINI

Doshtano?

MR. KEORA

Minna gakko nanka yori chaya ga ii soda.

SAKINI

They say they just held meeting in democratic fashion and ma-jority agree on resolution. They want you to build them cha ya.

FISBY

A what?

SAKINI

Cha ya. That's teahouse, boss.

FISBY

A teahouse?

SAKINI

Yes, boss. They say now that this village have geisha girl just like big city, they should have teahouse like big city too.

FISBY

But I can't build them a teahouse . . . I have no authority to do that.

SAKINI

But you tell them will of majority is law. You going to break law?

FISBY

They're going to get a school . . . that's enough.

SAKINI

But majority too old to go to school . . . they want teahouse.

FISBY

There is no provision in Plan B for a teahouse.

LOTUS BLOSSOM

Ano . . . ochaya sae tatereba mondai naija nai no.

SAKINI

Lotus Blossom say teahouse in Tobiki make recovery program work. Everybody make geta and cricket cages like crazy so they can spend money at teahouse.

FISBY

I haven't got any materials to build a teahouse.

SAKINI

Zairyo ga naiyo.

96

LOTUS BLOSSOM

Ara, kinoo renga ya zaimoku takusan kite orimashitayo.

SAKINI

She say Army truck come yesterday and leave beautiful brick and lovely paint.

FISBY

For the new *schoolhouse*. Tell them...it just can't be done.

SAKINI

Dame, dame, dame desuyo!
    (FISBY *looks down into the disappointed faces of the* VILLAGERS.)

VILLAGERS

Achara-san, iijiwaru dane.

SAKINI

They say you very mean to them after *all* the nice presents they give you.

FISBY

I'm sorry.

SAKINI

They very sorry too, boss. You know why?

FISBY

I think I do.

SAKINI

No, boss. When you leave here...Tobiki be forgotten village. Not have park, not have statue...not even lovely jail. Tobiki like to be proud. Teahouse give them face.

FISBY

It's going to be a fine schoolhouse. Five sides.

OSHIRA

May I speak, Captain-san?

FISBY

Of course, Mr. Oshira.

OSHIRA

There are lovely teahouses in the big cities. But the men of Tobiki have never been inside them. We are too poor and our clothes are too ragged. All of my life I have dreamed of visiting a teahouse where paper lanterns cast a light in the lotus pond and bamboo bells hanging in the pines tinkle as the breezes brush them. But this picture is only in my heart... I may never see it. I am an old man, sir. I shall die soon. It is evil for the soul to depart this world laden with envy or regret. Give us our teahouse, sir. Free my soul for death.

FISBY

(*Unhappily*)

But... we haven't got any carpenters!

SAKINI

(*Calls over the heads of the group*)

Oi! Daiku-san! Daiku-san!

(MR. SUMATA and HIS FATHER *come trotting across the stage carrying their carpenter boxes.* SAKINI *turns to* FISBY.)

Oh, what you think? Mr. Sumata and his papa just come down from mountains!

98

FISBY

(*Gives* SAKINI *a penetrating but defeated look*)
All right. All right! I haven't got a chance. I guess Uncle Sam is going into the teahouse business.
(*He turns and goes back into his office, followed by* LOTUS BLOSSOM. *He picks up Plan B.* SAKINI *announces the decision from the steps.*)

SAKINI

Cha ya, tatete iiyo!
(*There is an outburst of cheers from the* VILLAGERS. *It sounds very much like* "Fisby-san, Banzai, Uncle Sam, Banzai!" *Inside* FISBY *begins tearing up Plan B.* LOTUS BLOSSOM *kneels before him, geta in hand.* FISBY *extends his feet and smiles down at her. The cheering outside continues. As the panels descend—*

THE SCENE BLACKS OUT QUICKLY

Scene 2

SCENE: *Colonel Purdy's office.*

TIME: *Few weeks later.*

AT RISE: *The right panel is lifted. A light picks up* COLONEL PURDY. *He sits at his desk fuming over a report. The rest of the stage remains dark. He calls* GREGOVICH *on his office inter-com.*

PURDY
  Gregovich!

GREGOVICH'S VOICE
  Yes, sir?

PURDY
  Get me Captain Fisby at Tobiki.

GREGOVICH
  Yes, sir.
> (*The extreme left panel rises leaving the intervening panels lowered.* FISBY *sits with his feet propped up on his desk. He is wearing his bathrobe "kimono."* LOTUS BLOSSOM *stands at his side fanning him. Over the scene, the sound of hammering and sawing can be heard. Over this the phone can be heard to ring.* FISBY *lifts the receiver.*)

FISBY

Captain Fisby.

PURDY

Colonel Purdy.

FISBY

       (*Over noise*)

Who?

PURDY

Colonel Purdy!

FISBY

I can't hear you. Hold on a minute.
       (*He turns to* LOTUS BLOSSOM.)
See if you can stop that hammering on the teahouse for a
minute.
       (*He goes through the motions.* LOTUS BLOSSOM *nods
understandingly and goes out.*)

PURDY

What's going on down there, Fisby?

FISBY

       (*As the noises cease*)
Now, who is it?

PURDY

Colonel Purdy.

FISBY

       (*Wraps his robe about his legs quickly*)
Oh, good afternoon, Colonel.

PURDY

I want to talk to you about your Progress Report.

FISBY

I sent it in.

PURDY

I have it. I have it right in front of me. I've read it twice. Now, suppose *you* tell *me* what it says.

FISBY

What would you like to have me explain, sir?

PURDY

I'd like you to explain why there's nothing in here about the schoolhouse. Didn't you get the lumber?

FISBY

(*Uneasily*)

Yes, sir . . . it's being used right now. But we'll need some more, I'm afraid.

PURDY

I sent ample according to specifications. How big a structure are you building?

FISBY

Well . . . we ought to consider expansion. Populations increase.

PURDY

We don't need to consider expansion. Our troops will be out of here by the next generation. Which brings me to another point.

(*He refers to the report.*)

What's this about six kids being born last week?

102

FISBY

Well, there wasn't much else to fill the Progress Report, sir.

PURDY

Then you've failed at your indoctrination. Don't you know yet that births are entered under "Population Increases"? They are not considered progress.

FISBY

But they weren't children, sir. They were kids . . . goats.

PURDY

There must be something wrong with this connection. It sounded just as if you said "goats."

FISBY

I did, sir. Kids . . . goats. You see, we're trying to increase the livestock herd down here. I thought . . .

PURDY

Goats! I don't care what you thought. Look here, Fisby. Suppose some congressman flew in to inspect our team. How would I explain such a report?

FISBY

Well, goats will breed, sir. Congress can't stop that. And I've been concerned with . . .

PURDY

The population of civilians alone concerns us. I want to know exactly what progress you've made as outlined in Plan B.

FISBY

Well . . . I'm getting along fine with the people.

PURDY

In other words, nothing. Listen to me. Do you realize what Major McEvoy has accomplished in his village?

FISBY

No, sir.

PURDY

Well, I'll tell you. His fourth-graders know the alphabet through "M," and his whole village can sing "God Bless America" in English.

FISBY

Yes, sir. That's real progress, sir. I wish I could say the same.

PURDY

See that you do. I don't want any rotten apples in my barrel. Now...I want to know exactly what you have accomplished in the five weeks you've been down there.

FISBY

Well, sir...I've started an industry. I'm sending our first shipment out for sale this week.

PURDY

What are you making?

FISBY

(*Looks down at his feet*)
Oh, getas and...

PURDY

Wait a minute...what in God's name is a *geta?*

104

FISBY

Not "a" geta ... *getas* ... you have to have two.

PURDY

Are you breeding some *other* kind of animal?

FISBY

You wear them on your feet, sir. Excellent for strengthening the metatarsal muscles. Then ... I have a group busy building cricket cages. ...

PURDY

Captain Fisby!

FISBY

Yes, sir.

PURDY

What kind of cages did you say?

FISBY

Cricket. Like in cricket on the hearth. I think we'll find a great market for them. Of course, we don't supply the crickets.

PURDY

Naturally not. Captain Fisby ... have you been taking your salt pills?

FISBY

Yes, sir ... I take them at cha ya ... with my tea.

PURDY

Have you been going out in the sun without your helmet?

FISBY

I wear a kasa, sir ... it's more practical ... wind can blow through the straw.

PURDY
> I see. I see. That will be all, Captain.
> > (*He hangs up quickly.*)

FISBY
> Hello ... hello ...
> > (*He hangs up and sits looking at the phone rather puzzled. The lights go down in his office and the panel descends.* COLONEL PURDY *also sits looking at the phone in his office. He calls* SERGEANT GREGOVICH *on the inter-com.*)

PURDY
> Sergeant! What is the name of that psychiatrist over at Awasi?

GREGOVICH
> Captain McLean?

PURDY
> Get him on the phone. My man at Tobiki has gone completely off his rocker!

THE SCENE BLACKS OUT QUICKLY

Scene 3

SCENE: *Captain Fisby's office.*

TIME: *A few days later.*

AT RISE: *The office is empty as the panel rises. After a moment*
           CAPTAIN MC LEAN *enters. He is an intense, rather wild-
           eyed man in his middle forties. He glances about fur-
           tively, then begins to examine the papers on Fisby's
           desk. He makes several notes in a notebook. He picks
           up Fisby's cricket cage and is examining it intently
           when* FISBY *enters behind him. He halts upon seeing*
           MC LEAN. FISBY *is wearing his blue bathrobe, his geta
           and a native straw hat.*

FISBY
   Well, who are you?

MC LEAN
        (*Gasps in surprise*)
   Oh, you startled me.

FISBY
   Can I do anything for you? I'm Captain Fisby.

MC LEAN
   I'm Captain McLean. There was no one here . . . so I came in.

FISBY
        (*He looks at his insignia.*)
   Oh, medical corps. What brings you to Tobiki?

MC LEAN

Well, I'm—I'm on leave. Thought I'd spend it making some—some—ethnological studies.

> (*He adds quickly*)

Of the natives.

FISBY

Well, you couldn't have come to a more interesting spot. Sit down, Captain.

MC LEAN

> (*Sits*)

Thank you. Would you have any objection to my spending a week or so making my studies, Captain?

FISBY

Not at all. Make yourself at home. I'll take that if it's in your way.

> (*He reaches out to relieve* MC LEAN *of the cricket cage he still holds.*)

MC LEAN

> (*Glances at the cage in his hand and laughs awkwardly.*)

Oh, yes. I was just examining it.

FISBY

> (*Pleased at his authority on the subject*)

It's a cricket cage.

MC LEAN

> (*Pauses*)

You ... like crickets?

FISBY

I haven't found one yet. But at least I've got the cage. I've got two . . . if you want one.

MC LEAN

Thank you, no. Thank you very much.
(*He looks at* FISBY's *attire.*)
What happened to your uniform, Captain?

FISBY

It's around. I find getas and a kimono much more comfortable in this climate.

MC LEAN

But isn't that a bathrobe?

FISBY

(*Shrugs*)
It passes for a kimono. Would you like to take off your shoes, Captain?

MC LEAN

Thank you . . . no. I'll keep them on if you don't mind.

FISBY

Can I offer you some tsukemono? You eat these during the day between meals.
(*He extends a platter.*)
Tsukemono means fragrant things.

MC LEAN

I just had a chocolate bar, thank you.
(*He rises and looks out the door.*)
May I ask what you're building down the road?

109

FISBY

> (*Proudly*)

That's my cha ya.

> (*He pops a few tsukemonos into his mouth.*)

It's really going to be something to write home about.

MC LEAN

Cha ya?

FISBY

Well, it just so happens, Captain, that I own a geisha girl. That might sound strange to you, but you get used to these things after a while. And if you have a geisha, you've got to have a cha ya. Sure you don't want some tsukemono?

MC LEAN

I really couldn't eat a thing.

> (*He glances out the door again.*)

May I ask what the men are doing down there wading in that irrigation ditch?

FISBY

They're not wading, they're building a lotus pond. You can't have a cha ya without a lotus pond.

MC LEAN

> (*Sits opposite* FISBY)

How have you felt lately, Fisby?

FISBY

McLean, I'll tell you something. I've never been happier. I feel reckless and free. And it all happened the moment I decided not to build that damned pentagon-shaped school.

MC LEAN
That what?

FISBY
The good colonel ordered me to build a pentagon-shaped schoolhouse down here. But the people wanted a teahouse. Believe it or not, someone gave me a geisha girl. So I'm giving this village what it wants. That must all sound pretty crazy to you, Mac.

MC LEAN
Well, yes and no.

FISBY
These are wonderful people with a strange sense of beauty. And hard-working . . . when there's a purpose. You should have seen them start out day before yesterday, great bundles of things they'd made piled high on their heads. Getas, cricket cages, lacquer ware—things to sell as souvenirs up north. Don't let anyone tell you these people are lazy.

MC LEAN
Oh. I see. I see.

FISBY
No, you don't. But you'll have a chance to study them.

MC LEAN
So you're building them a teahouse.

FISBY
Next thing I'm going to do for them is find out if this land here will grow anything besides sweet potatoes. I'm going to send for fertilizers and DDT and—

MC LEAN

> (*Leaps to his feet*)

Chemicals!

FISBY

Sure, why not?

MC LEAN

Do you want to poison these people?

FISBY

No, but—

MC LEAN

Now you've touched on a subject that is very close to me. For years I've planned to retire and buy a farm—raise specialties for big restaurants. So let me tell you this. Chemicals will kill all your earthworms, and earthworms aerate your soil.

FISBY

They do?

MC LEAN

Do you know an earthworm leaves castings eight times its own weight every day?

FISBY

That much!

MC LEAN

Organic gardening is the only thing. Nature's way—compost, manure, but no chemicals.

FISBY

Hey! You know a lot about this.

MC LEAN

(*Modestly*)

I should. I've subscribed to all the farm journals for years.

FISBY

Say, you could help these people out while you're here—if you would. Do you think you could take over supervision—establish a sort of experimental station for them?

MC LEAN

Well, I—no—no—I haven't time.

FISBY

Take time. This is a chance for you to put some of your theories into practice.

MC LEAN

(*Haughtily*)

They are not theories. They are proven facts.

FISBY

I'll give you a couple of men to help, and all you'd have to do is tell us how.

MC LEAN

(*Hesitates*)

Is your soil acid or alkaline?

FISBY

Gosh, I don't know.

MC LEAN

Well, that's the very *first* thing you have to find out. Do you have bees?

FISBY

I haven't seen any.

MC LEAN

(*Shakes his head sadly*)

People always underestimate the importance of bees for pollinating.

FISBY

(*Slaps him on the back*)

Mac, you're just the man we've needed down here. You're a genius!

MC LEAN

I'll want plenty of manure.

FISBY

You'll get it.

MC LEAN

And I'll want to plan this program scientifically. I wish I had some of my books . . . and my seed catalogues.

(*He measures from the floor.*)

I've got a stack of catalogues that high.

FISBY

Why don't you make a list, and I'll get the boys over at the airstrip to fly us in seeds from the States.

MC LEAN

> (*The gardener fever possesses the doctor as he begins to make his list.*)

Every spring I've made lists of seeds and never had any soil to put them in. And now . . . I could actually germinate.

> (*He writes*)

Corn—Golden Bantam.

> (*Then adds enthusiastically*)

And Country Gentleman! Hybrid.

FISBY

Why don't I just leave you with your list while I check on the lotus pond?

> (MC LEAN *doesn't hear him.*)

Well, I'll be back for tea. We have tea in the pine grove and watch the sun go down.

> (*He goes out*)

MC LEAN

> (*Continues with his list reading aloud*)

Cucumbers—Extra Early Green Prolific.

> (*His enthusiasm mounts.*)

Radishes—Crimson Giant!

> (*The telephone begins to ring; he ignores it as he writes.*)

Tomatoes—Ponderosa Earliana.

> (*The telephone rings insistently.*)

Watermelon!

> (*He closes his eyes ecstatically.*)
> (*The panel rises on the opposite side of the stage revealing Colonel Purdy's office. The intervening panel remains down.* COLONEL PURDY *sits at his desk jiggling his telephone hook.*)

PURDY

What's the matter with this connection! Ring again!

MC LEAN
> (*Ignores the ringing*)

Watermelon—All-American Gold Medal!
> (*He writes it down as the phone rings. He looks up impatiently and lifts the receiver.*)

Hello!

PURDY
> (*Confidentially*)

Who is this?

MC LEAN

This is Captain McLean.

PURDY

This is Colonel Purdy. Can you talk?

MC LEAN

Why not?

PURDY

I was anxious to hear your report on you-know-who.

MC LEAN

On *who?*

PURDY

Captain Fisby! The man I sent you down to examine.

MC LEAN

Oh.
> (*He weighs his problem quickly.*)

Oh. Well . . . I'll have to stay down here several weeks for
some . . .

PURDY
Several weeks!

MC LEAN
Rome wasn't built in a day.

PURDY
What?

MC LEAN
I said, Rome wasn't built in a day.

PURDY
(*Digests this*)
Well ... you're the doctor.

MC LEAN
I'll send in a report ... from time to time. I can tell you now
I expect to work miracles down here.

PURDY
Splendid ... splendid. Is there anything I can send? Some old
Adventure Magazines or anything?

MC LEAN
There are a couple of books I'd like, but I don't think you could
get them.

PURDY
(*Picks up pencil*)
You name them.

MC LEAN
Well ... one is *Principles of Pea Production*, and the other is
Do's and Don'ts of Cabbage Culture.
(PURDY *starts to write ... then stops.*)
And do you think you could lay your hands on a soil test kit?

PURDY
> (*Looks at earphone*)
A what?

MC LEAN
> (*Enunciating*)
A *soil test kit*. I want to see if the soil is sour down here.

PURDY
Sour, did you say?

MC LEAN
Yes... if your soil is sour your seeds won't germinate. And I sure wish I had some bees.

PURDY
There *is* something wrong with this connection!

MC LEAN
I'm going to take time out here to build up the soil with manure.

PURDY
> (*Unbelieving*)
Did you say manure?

MC LEAN
I've lost faith in chemicals. You kill all your worms. I can tell you, when you kill a worm, Colonel... you're killing a friend.
> (*There is a long pause.*)
Hello... hello.

PURDY
> (*Puts down the phone and turns to the squawk box.*)
Gregovich, where is Plan B!

GREGOVICH'S VOICE
What did you want, sir?

PURDY
I want to see who I send to analyze an analyst.

THE PANELS FALL QUICKLY ON EACH SIDE
OF THE STAGE

Scene 4

SCENE: *Village square.*

TIME: *Few weeks later.*

AT RISE: *The panels rise to reveal the village square and Fisby's office. Natives are seated in the square, great bundles beside them. Others arrive and sink into positions of dejection.* FISBY *works at his desk.* SAKINI *enters and looks at the* VILLAGERS.

SAKINI
   (*To* MR. KEORA)
Doshtano?

KEORA
Hitotsu mo unremasenna.

SAKINI
   Oh, oh ... too bad.
      (SAKINI *crosses and enters Fisby's office.*)
   Boss!

FISBY
   Yes?

SAKINI
   Mr. Keora and everybody back from Big Koza.

FISBY

Good. Let's see how they made out.
> (*He steps outside followed by* SAKINI. *He stops as he sees his* VILLAGERS *sitting dejectedly before their large bundles. He turns to* SAKINI.)
What's the matter?

SAKINI

Mr. Keora very tired. Walk two days with bundle on back to sell straw hats to American soldiers at Big Koza. Nobody buy, so walk back. Too many damn hats now, boss.

FISBY

He couldn't sell *any?*
> (SAKINI *shakes his head.*)
Why not?

SAKINI

> (*Shrugs*)
Soldiers not want. Soldiers say ... what you think we are ... hayseed? So come home.

FISBY

> (*Sees old* MR. OSHIRA *and crosses to him.* OSHIRA *rises.*)
Mr. Oshira ... did you take your lacquer ware to Yatoda?

OSHIRA

Oh, yes ... but come back ... not go again.

FISBY

But I don't understand.... The Navy always spends money.

OSHIRA

Sailors say, "Oh, pretty good ... how much you want?" I say, "Twenty-five yen." They say, "Oh, too much ... can get better in five-and-ten-cent store. Give you one nickel."

FISBY

Did you explain how many years it took you to learn how to turn out such work?

OSHIRA

(*Nods*)
They say, "What you want us to do, cry?"

FISBY

(*Angrily*)
Damn stupid morons!
(*He turns back to* OSHIRA.)
Did you tell them that each cup was handmade?

OSHIRA

They say ... not care. They say ... at home have big machines that turn out ten cups every minute. They say ... take nickel or jump in lake.

FISBY

(*Unhappily*)
So you had to carry them all the way back?

SAKINI

Poor Mr. Oshira. No one want his lacquer ware.

FISBY

Well, he's wrong. He's a great artist and I'll buy everything he's made myself.

SAKINI

But you not able to buy everything from everybody in Tobiki, boss.

122

FISBY

(*Sits down on steps*)
Tell them that they should all be proud of their work. And
that I'm proud of all of them.

SAKINI

Gokro, gokro san.

FISBY

I'll think of something . . . I'll hit on an idea to bring money to
this village yet.

SAKINI

Boss . . . you stop work on teahouse now?

FISBY

No! You'll get a teahouse if I give you nothing else.

SAKINI

They sure wish they could make some money to spend at teahouse, boss. Not like to go like beggars.

FISBY

Give me a little time, Sakini.
(*As they sit around, each deep in his personal problems,*
MC LEAN *enters. His uniform is gone. He is wearing his*
bathrobe, a straw hat and geta.)

MC LEAN

Fisby! You're just the man I want to see. Can I have a couple
of boys to help me? The damn Japanese beetles are eating up
my Chinese peas.

FISBY

(*Dispiritedly*)
Sure . . . I'll get a couple for you.

MC LEAN
>   (*Looks around*)
> What's the matter?

FISBY
> There's no market for our products.

MC LEAN
> Oh ... that's too bad. What are you going to do?
>   (*He sits down.*)

FISBY
> Try to think of something.

OSHIRA
> The world has left us behind.
>   (*The* VILLAGERS *begin to rise and pick up their handi-work.*)

SEIKO
> Amerika-san no seija naiyo. Sa, sa, kaette yakezake da!

SAKINI
> They say ... tell you not your fault no one wants to buy, boss.
> They say guess they go home now and get drunk.

FISBY
> Tell them I don't blame them. If I had anything to drink ...
> I'd do the same.
>   (*As they start to file out, both* MC LEAN *and* FISBY *have a delayed reaction. They leap to their feet together.*)
> Wait a minute!
>   (*The* VILLAGERS *stop.*)
> What are they going to get drunk *on?*

SAKINI

They got nothing but brandy.

MC LEAN

Nothing but *brandy!*

FISBY

How did they manage to get brandy?

SAKINI

We make very fine brandy here, from sweet potatoes. Been making for generations.

FISBY

You make a brandy *yourselves?*

SAKINI

Oh, yes. We make for weddings and funerals.

FISBY

      (*Looks at* MC LEAN)
What does it taste like?

SAKINI

You want some, boss?
      (*He turns to* HOKAIDA.)
Imozake, skoshi!

FISBY

Sakini, if this stuff is any good at all, we're in business. This is one thing I *know* our men will buy.

SAKINI

Oh...I think we not like to sell brandy. Only make for cere-mony.

125

MC LEAN

It may not be any good anyhow. There are some things even the troops won't drink.

HOKAIDA

(*Returns with an earthen jug*)

Hai, imozake.

(*He hands the jug to* FISBY)

SAKINI

There you are, boss. You like taste now?

FISBY

I'd like to smell it first.

(*He gives it a sniff and jerks his head back.*)

MC LEAN

Obviously, it has a kick.

FISBY

How old is this brandy, Sakini?

SAKINI

(*Turns to Hokaida*)

Kore itsuno?

HOKAIDA

(*Holds up seven fingers*)

Issukan mae dayo.

FISBY

Seven years old?

SAKINI

Oh, no, boss. He make last week.

FISBY

It couldn't smell like that in only a week.

SAKINI

Is village secret. You try now?

FISBY

(*Hands it to* MC LEAN)
You try it, Mac. You're a medical man.

MC LEAN

(*Backs away*)
You first.

FISBY

I insist. You're my guest.

MC LEAN

I waive the honor.

FISBY

(*Turns to* SAKINI)
Has anyone ever gone blind or died from this?

MC LEAN

He said they make it for funerals.

SAKINI

Oh, no, boss. We not blind. We not dead.

FISBY

There, you see.

MC LEAN

They've worked up an immunity over the years.

FISBY

Well, I don't want to kill any of my countrymen. Couldn't you make some sort of test, Doc?
> (*As* MC LEAN *considers this, the bleat of a goat is heard offstage.* FISBY *and* MC LEAN *exchange looks and nod.*)

Sakini, get Lady Astor.
> (*To* MC LEAN)

That's Miss Higa Jiga's goat. She asked me to give it a classy name.
> (SAKINI *goes to get* LADY ASTOR.)

MC LEAN

I'm not sure what we'll prove. Goats have hardy stomachs.

SAKINI

> (*Returns leading a goat*)

Boss, you make guinea pig of goat?

FISBY

If this passes the goat-test, it's all right. No Marine would ever admit he had a weaker stomach than a goat.

MC LEAN

May I borrow this a moment?
> (*He takes* MR. HOKAIDA's *red helmet and pours into it from the jug.*)

SAKINI

Lady Astor very lucky goat.

128

FISBY

You hold her, Sakini. Proceed, Doctor . . . in the name of science.
(*The goat sniffs the contents of the helmet.*)
We're either going to have an industry or goat meat for dinner.
(LADY ASTOR *begins to drink the concoction. They watch her lap up the liquor and lick her lips with relish.*)

MC LEAN

(*Stands back*)
It doesn't seem to affect her.
(*Draws his fingers back and forth in front of the goat's eyes*)
Reflexes all right.

FISBY

Let's watch her a minute. The future of Tobiki and the health of the Army are at stake here.
(FISBY *and* MC LEAN *and the* VILLAGERS *stand watching the goat.* LADY ASTOR *is quite content.* FISBY *rises.*)
Well, here goes.
(*He takes the jug and samples the contents himself.* MC LEAN *watches him. Then he, too, tests from the jug. They look at each other and grin.*)
Whee!
(*He dashes for his office.*)

SAKINI

(*Follows*)
What you going to do, boss?

FISBY

I am about to form the Cooperative Brewing Company of Tobiki.
(FISBY *is followed by* SAKINI, MC LEAN, *and some of the* VILLAGERS. *He picks up the phone.*)
Get me the Officers' Club at Awasi.

SAKINI

We going to make brandy, boss?

FISBY

I'll tell you in a minute.

(*He turns back to telephone.*)

Hello ... Officers' Club, Awasi? This is Captain Fisby at Tobiki. Oh, hello, Major, how are you? Major, when I was with your unit, you could never keep a supply of liquor in the club, and I stumbled onto something and wondered if you'd be interested. Tobiki, as you know, is the heart of the brandy industry and—

(*He takes the phone away from his ear as the word brandy is shouted back at him.*)

Yes ... brandy....

(*He turns to* MC LEAN)

Doc, look up the word "sweet potato" and see if it has another fancier name.

(*He turns back to the phone.*)

Yes ... I'm here ... yes ... I could get you some if you could pay their price and keep the source secret. Oh, yes, it's been made here for generations. Why, you never tasted anything like it.

MC LEAN

The Haitian word for sweet potato is *b-a-t-a-t-a*.

(*He spells it out.*)

FISBY

(*Into the phone*)

You've heard of Seven Star Batata, haven't you? Well, Tobiki is where it's made.

(*He turns to* MC LEAN)

The Seven Star did it.

130

SAKINI

Brandy much better if eight or ten days old, boss.

FISBY

We also have Eight Star and Ten Star. Well, naturally the Ten
Star comes a little higher. It sells for—
      (*He looks at* SAKINI *desperately.* SAKINI *holds up ten
      fingers.*)
A hundred occupation yen a gallon.

SAKINI

I mean *ten* yen, boss.

FISBY

Delivered. All right, we'll send up five gallons in about a week.
It'll be delivered by our Department of Agriculture. You're
welcome.
      (*He hangs up and turns to* SAKINI.)
Sakini, if every family in Tobiki starts making brandy, how
much can we turn out in a week?

SAKINI

Oh, maybe . . . forty . . . fifty gallons.

FISBY

Better aim for eighty.
      (*He lifts the receiver again.*)
I'd like to get the naval base at Big Koza, Officers' Club, Commander Myers.

SAKINI

Maybe if everybody build private stills, Tobiki can turn out
hundred gallon.

FISBY

I'll know better after I talk to the Navy.

(*He speaks into the phone.*)

Commander Myers? Captain Fisby at Tobiki. Commander, we've got a surplus of brandy down here and I was wondering...

(*Again he takes the phone away from his ear as the word brandy is blasted back.*)

Yes. Brandy. Ten Star Batata. Well, Lady Astor won't drink anything else. Oh... we could supply you with as much as you want at a hundred yen a gallon. Fifteen gallons? Right! It will be delivered Horse Cart Special in ten days.

(*He hangs up and turns to the others crowding into his office.*)

Sakini, tell them to all start making brandy, and in a week or two everyone in this village is going to have more money than he ever dreamed of.

SAKINI

Ah, dondon kaseide sake tsukreba minna kanega mokaruyo!

MR. KEORA

Minna shiroi koto katte moii darone?

SAKINI

They say... if they work like the dickens, can they all have white coats like the mayor?

FISBY

Yes. I'll get the cloth somewhere. That's a promise.

(*The telephone rings.*)

Wait a minute. Hello? Well, word gets around fast.

(*He picks up his order blank.*)

Twenty gallons? PX, GHQ, C.O.D. O.K.

(*He hangs up*)

Get to work, boys!
>   (*As they turn to leave,* FISBY *suddenly leaps to his feet.*)

Wait!
>   (*They stand frozen as he crouches and starts toward them. He slaps his hand on the floor and then rises triumphantly.*)

I got my cricket!
>   (*The* VILLAGERS *cheer for* FISBY.)

THE PANELS FALL QUICKLY

ACT THREE

Scene I

SCENE: *Teahouse of the August Moon.*

TIME: *Several weeks later.*

AT RISE: *All the panels are down.* SAKINI *steps from the wings
to address the audience.*

SAKINI
  (Bows)
Ability of Americans for mass production equaled only by
  American capacity for consumption.
Fortune often comes in back door while we look out front
  window.
Prosperity not only smile on Tobiki.
Prosperity giggle like silly girl.
Very strange.
Things we do best . . . not wanted.
Things we think least of . . . wanted most.
No conclusion.
Tobiki now village of beautiful houses.
But loveliest of all is Teahouse of August Moon.
  *(He goes off extreme left, signaling for the panels to rise.
  Offstage the music of string instruments can be heard
  playing softly. The panels go up. The ugly thatched huts
  are gone. In the center of the stage, exquisite in its
  simplicity, stands the teahouse. Small bells tinkle from
  its pagoda roof. Soft lights glow through the colored
  paper panels. Dwarf pines edge the walk leading to a*

137

*small bridge. An August moon hangs in the autumn sky.
The silhouette of* LOTUS BLOSSOM *is framed in the center
panel by the soft back lighting. She slides the panel open
and steps into the almost bare center room of the teahouse. She crosses and lights the lanterns hanging from
the eave extensions. As she goes through this ceremony,
the* GUESTS *wander in. Before they enter the teahouse,
they remove their shoes and rinse their fingers in the
ceremonial bamboo basin. Then they enter and seat
themselves on green floor mats. The* WOMEN *are dressed
in silk kimonos of varying hues and the majority of the
men wear spotless white suits.* LOTUS BLOSSOM *bows to
them and returns through the sliding door again.* FISBY
and MC LEAN, *followed by* SAKINI, *enter.* SAKINI *wears a
white suit and the* AMERICANS *wear their bathrobes and
geta. They are greeted enthusiastically by the* GUESTS.)

SAKINI

I tell Lotus Blossom you here, boss.
(*He disappears through the sliding panel in the center
of the teahouse.*)

FISBY

(*As they walk around inspecting the grounds*)
It's really something, isn't it?

MC LEAN

Where did they all get their white suits?

FISBY

They made them.

MC LEAN

Where'd they get the cloth?

138

FISBY

I got it from the naval base at Awasi for ten gallons of brandy.
It's target cloth.

MC LEAN

Those kimonos aren't target cloth.

FISBY

Parachute silk. Six gallons' worth.
> (LOTUS BLOSSOM *enters, followed by* SAKINI. *She hurries
> down to* FISBY *and bows. She extends a yellow chrys-
> anthemum to him.*)

SAKINI

Chrysanthemum bud in full bloom, boss.

LOTUS BLOSSOM

> (*She bows as* FISBY *accepts the gift.*)
Hop-pee.
> (*Her eyes almost disappear in a great smile of pride.*)

FISBY

What did she say?

SAKINI

I try like the dickens to teach her to say "happy birthday," but
she can't say "birthday," boss.

LOTUS BLOSSOM

Hop-pee.

FISBY

Well...I'm floored!
> (*He bows to her.*)
Thank you, Lotus Blossom.
> (*To* SAKINI)
How did you know?

MC LEAN

I gave you away.

SAKINI

Everybody in village like to show appreciation, boss.

FISBY

I should have had a kimono made. When you said "formal," I thought this would do.

LOTUS BLOSSOM

Hop-pee. Hop-pee.

FISBY

And a hop-pee hop-pee to you.

GUESTS

(*Murmur in the background*)
Hayaku oiwai hajimeyo, soda, soda.

SAKINI

Everybody impatient to get on with the party, boss.

LOTUS BLOSSOM

Hop-pee.
(*She indicates the center mat.*)

SAKINI

You sit down now, boss. Lotus Blossom going to dance in your honor.

FISBY

You hear that.... She's going to dance!
(*Quickly sits down*)
Sit down, you farmer.... This is in my honor.

140

MC LEAN

My, my! How am I going to stall Purdy so I can stay down here?

FISBY

I'll have a relapse for you.
> (*They turn to watch* LOTUS BLOSSOM *as she takes her position and the first notes are struck by the musicians present.* LOTUS BLOSSOM *performs for them a traditional dance of infinite grace and delicacy. She finishes, concluding her performance in front of* FISBY, *who rises and bows to her.*)

What a lovely little thing you are! This belongs to you.
> (*He returns the chrysanthemum with a flourish.* LOTUS BLOSSOM *accepts it and seats herself quickly on a mat and hides her head.*)

SAKINI

Oh, boss ... you know what you do!

FISBY

It called for flowers.

SAKINI

That mean you give your heart to her.

FISBY

> (*Lightly*)

Well, I do. We all do.
> (*Turns to* MC LEAN)

Wasn't that beautiful, Mac!

MC LEAN

She can dance in my cha ya any day.

SAKINI

You sit beside Lotus Blossom now, boss. You guest of honor and referee.

FISBY

(*Starts to sit down*)
Referee! I thought this was a birthday party.

SAKINI

Lotus Blossom now putting on wrestling match for you, boss.

FISBY

Wrestling match?

LOTUS BLOSSOM

(*Stands and claps hands*)
Sa, osumo hajime mashoyo.
(*Immediately two men bring in four poles which they set up downstage center to mark a square. Each pole has colored cloth hanging from it.*)

MC LEAN

Who is wrestling?
(*He sits next to* FISBY.)

SAKINI

Wrestling match between Chief of Agriculture and Chief of Police.

FISBY

(*To* LOTUS BLOSSOM)
Hokaida and Seiko?
(*She nods.*)

SAKINI

Grudge fight, boss.

142

FISBY

Really?

SAKINI

Whoever win match get to haul sweet potatoes for Lotus
Blossom.

FISBY

(*Watching the poles being set up, he indicates them to*
LOTUS BLOSSOM.)
Why have they wrapped colored cloth around the poles?

LOTUS BLOSSOM

Kuro wa fuyu, Ao wa haru, Akaga natsu de, Shirowa akiyo.
Wakkatta?

SAKINI

She explain, boss, that black cloth remind us of winter, green
cloth remind us of spring, red is the summer and white the
autumn.

LOTUS BLOSSOM

(*Claps her hands*)
Osumo, osumo!
(MR. HOKAIDA, *bare except for a pair of black shorts,*
enters and crosses to one corner of the ring, where he
squats on his heels. An outburst of approval greets his
entrance. He smiles with fatuous pleasure, and makes a
desperate effort to hold in his fat stomach.)

MC LEAN

Do his black shorts mean anything?

SAKINI

Just easy to clean.

> (LOTUS BLOSSOM *claps her dainty hands again.* MR. SEIKO *enters, lean and wiry, also wearing black shorts and a sweat shirt reading* U.S.S. Princeton.)

FISBY

Where did he get *that?*

SAKINI

Sailor at naval base. Some class, eh?

> (MR. SEIKO *peels off the shirt to great applause and squats in the opposite corner. He glares across at* HOKAIDA, *who thrusts his jaw forward.*)

They waiting on you to give signal now, boss.

FISBY

Waiting on *me?*

SAKINI

Oh, yes . . . you are Honorable Referee.

LOTUS BLOSSOM

> (*Hands her fan to* FISBY)

Korede aizu shite kudasai.

FISBY

What do I do with this?

SAKINI

Now you cover face with fan.

FISBY

Why?

SAKINI

That mean you not take sides. Now you go to center of ring and drop fan from face.

MC LEAN

And get the hell out in a hurry.

FISBY

How many falls?

SAKINI

No falls, boss. First one to throw other out of ring—winner.
(FISBY *covers his face with the fan and walks down center. The two wrestlers crouch, poised to leap, their eyes on the fan.* FISBY *whips the fan away from his face and dashes back out of range. The protagonists circle each other slowly. Suddenly all hell breaks loose. The teahouse guests cheer their favorite. The fat* MR. HOKAIDA *picks up* MR. SEIKO *and subjects him to a series of head spins and thumpings. But he exhausts himself; and it is* SEIKO *who ends by tossing* HOKAIDA *out of the ring. A cheer rises from the guests.* FISBY *sighs with relief.*)
Now the judges must decide who win.

FISBY

Decide! Is there any doubt?
(*The three judges confer. They then turn to* MR. HOKAIDA *and bow.*)

SAKINI

Mr. Hokaida! The winner...
(*This startling announcement is greeted with approval.* SEIKO *beats his head and wails.*)

FISBY

How *could* he be the winner! He was thrown out of the ring.

145

SAKINI
Maybe so, but judges all cousins of Mr. Hokaida.

FISBY
But the judges are wrong.

SAKINI
(*Confidentially*)
We know who really win...but this way nobody lose face.
(SEIKO *and* HOKAIDA *exit.*)

LOTUS BLOSSOM
Sa kondo wa Fu-san no ban yo.

SAKINI
Lotus Blossom say guests now wish *you* to perform.

FISBY
Perform what?

SAKINI
They like now for you and doctor to sing song or something.

FISBY
Sing!

SAKINI
Must do, boss. Bad manners to refuse.

FISBY
(*Repeats in alarm*)
Sing!
(*He turns to* MC LEAN.)
Get on your feet, Mac, we've got to sing something.
146

MC LEAN

What?

FISBY

We could sing the national anthem.

MC LEAN

No, we couldn't—I don't know the words.

FISBY

How about "Deep in the Heart of Texas"?

MC LEAN

Why not? There're no Texans here.
    (*They step forward.*)

FISBY

Mac, let's have some fun.
    (*He turns to* SAKINI.)
Sakini, you tell them they must all help us. They must clap
and sing "Deep in the Heart of Texas" every time *we* do.

SAKINI

    (*Beaming*)
Tewo tataite Deep in the Heart of Texas.
    (*Demonstrates clapping*)
Koshte, Deep in the Heart of Texas.
    (*The* VILLAGERS *chatter and agree with enthusiasm.* FISBY
    and MC LEAN *stand close together and begin singing. Each
    time they come to the designated phrase,* SAKINI *gives a
    signal and the* VILLAGERS *join in lustily. Lost in their
    eager concentration, no one observes the entrance of*
    COLONEL PURDY. *He looks from the "kimono"-clad figures
    of* FISBY *and* MC LEAN *to the assemblage. As he shouts at*
    FISBY, *his voice is drowned out by the chorus of "Deep
    in the Heart of Texas." The song continues.* PURDY

signals offstage. GREGOVICH *enters and is instructed by* COLONEL PURDY *to end the objectionable noises.*)

GREGOVICH

Captain Fisby!

> (*Again the voice coincides with the shouts of "Deep in the Heart of Texas" and is lost.* COLONEL PURDY *stalks downstage center, followed by* GREGOVICH.)

PURDY

Captain Fisby! What in the name of Occupation is going on here?

> (FISBY *gasps and backs away. Suddenly aware of his bathrobe, he stoops down to cover his bare legs.* MC LEAN *surrenders completely to panic. He runs to hide behind guests. The* GUESTS, *alarmed by the sudden intrusion, scatter in all directions. In the midst of this bedlam—*

THE PANELS ARE LOWERED

Scene 2

SCENE: *Office of Captain Fisby.*

TIME: *Next morning.*

AT RISE: *The four bamboo panels are down.* SAKINI *enters from the wings right and crosses down to the footlights.*

SAKINI
> (*Bows*)
When present is blackest,
Future can only be brighter.
Okinawa invaded many times.
Not sink in ocean yet.
Survive Chinese.
Survive Japanese.
Survive missionaries and Americans.
Invaded by typhoon.
Invaded by locust.
Invaded by cockroach and sweet-potato moth.
Tobiki now invaded by Honorable Colonel.
Not sink in ocean.
> (*He goes to the left side of the stage and raises the panels in front of Fisby's office. He then exits.* COLONEL PURDY *is seated at Fisby's desk going through his papers.* FISBY *stands behind him nervously watching.* MC LEAN *sits on the cot biting his nails. He rises.*)

149

PURDY

> (*Without looking up*)

Sit down!

> (MC LEAN *sits down again.* PURDY *turns to* FISBY *and glares at him.*)

Where are your bimonthly Progress Reports?

FISBY

I—I think they should be right here under the cricket cage, sir.

PURDY

> (*Takes some papers from under the cage and glances at them*)

These are all completely blank.

> (*He turns to* FISBY.)

Fisby, you can't convince me that you've been down here for two months doing absolutely nothing.

FISBY

Oh, no, sir. I mean yes, sir, I have not been doing "nothing."

PURDY

You're beginning to sound like a native.

MC LEAN

> (*Rises*)

The tendency is always to descend to the level of the environment, sir. It's a primary postulate of psychology.

PURDY

> (*Turns on him*)

Well, it's a primary regulation of the Army to make out reports!

> (*Back to* FISBY)

Now, I want to know exactly what you've accomplished here from the moment you arrived.

FISBY

Well, let me think....

MC LEAN

Could I—

FISBY

Sit down!
(*He turns to* FISBY.)
How many lectures have you delivered to the village children on democratic theory?

FISBY

Well, let me see.

PURDY

Four—five?

FISBY

(*Thinks*)
Not that many, sir.

PURDY

Three?

MC LEAN

(*Hopefully*)
Two?

FISBY

N-no.

PURDY

You only delivered *one* lecture?

FISBY

None, sir.

PURDY

Don't tell me you haven't delivered a single lecture!

FISBY

Yes, sir, I haven't delivered no lecture. I mean . . . any lecture.

PURDY

Did you organize a Ladies' League for Democratic Action?

FISBY

(*Beaming*)
Yes, sir. I sure did. I did that all right!

PURDY

And how many lectures on democratic theory have you given *them?*

FISBY

(*Deflated again*)
None, sir.

PURDY

You can't mean none. You must mean one or two.

FISBY

No, sir, none.

PURDY

I refuse to believe it.

FISBY

I'm glad, sir.

152

MC LEAN
> (*Rises in desperation*)

Sir, I *must* go.

PURDY

Where!

MC LEAN

My *seedlings* are wilting. I have to transplant them.

PURDY

Captain, you will pack your gear and transplant yourself to your unit at once.

MC LEAN

Yes, sir.
> (*He turns to* FISBY.)

They'll die. It's murder.
> (*He goes to the door and turns sadly to* FISBY *again.*)

Please take care of my beans.
> (*He exits.*)

PURDY
> (*Turns back to* FISBY)

Now! Is the schoolhouse finished?

FISBY
> (*Sighs*)

No, sir.

PURDY

Why isn't it finished?

FISBY

It isn't finished, sir, because it isn't started.

PURDY

I have a splitting headache, Fisby. I ask you not to provoke me needlessly. Now, where is the schoolhouse?

FISBY

I never built it.

PURDY

Don't stand there and tell me you never built it. I sent the lumber down two months ago.

FISBY

(*Impressed*)
Is it *that* long, sir?

PURDY

What did you do with the lumber I sent?

FISBY

Well, I built a teahouse.

PURDY

(*Stares at him*)
I don't suppose you have any aspirin here?

FISBY

No, sir, I haven't.

PURDY

Now, sit down. Fisby. I want to be fair.
(FISBY *sits down.*)
I'm a patient man. When I run into something that defies reason, I like to find the reason.
(*Explodes*)
What in the name of Occupation do you mean by saying you built a *teahouse* instead of a *schoolhouse!*

154

FISBY

It's a little hard to explain, sir. Everybody in the village wanted one . . . and Lotus Blossom needed it for her work.

PURDY

And just what is your relationship with this woman?

FISBY

Well, she was a present. So to speak. She's a geisha girl—after a fashion.

PURDY

You built this teahouse—this place for her to ply her trade—with lumber belonging to the Army of Occupation of the United States Government?

FISBY

Well, it just seemed like lumber at the time.

PURDY

Fisby, are you operating a house of prostitution here on Government rice?

FISBY

No, sir! Geishas aren't what you think.

PURDY

Don't tell me what to think. Army Intelligence warned me I'd find something mighty peculiar going on in Tobiki.

FISBY

What's Army Intelligence got to do with it, sir?

PURDY

You're not very cunning, Fisby. With all the Occupation money on the island finding its way to this village, did you think it wouldn't come to the attention of Intelligence?

FISBY

Oh.

PURDY

Why did you do it, Fisby, why!

FISBY

Well, Lotus Blossom had to have a place to teach the Ladies'
League how to become geishas and—

PURDY

Fisby! You mean to say you've turned all the decent women of
this village into professional...
(He slumps into the chair.)
How could you sink to such depths, man!

FISBY

I was only giving in to what the majority wanted, sir.

PURDY

I don't doubt that statement—not at all. It is a sad thing that it
took a war to convince me that most of the human race is de-
generate. Thank God I come from a country where the air is
clean, where the wind is fresh, where—

FISBY

(Interrupts)
For heaven's sake, sir, would you please listen to me instead of
yourself! There is not a thing goes on in that teahouse that
your mother couldn't watch.

PURDY

(Leaps to his feet and points a warning finger)
You be careful how you use my mother's name, Fisby.

156

FISBY

Well, *my* mother then. I swear there's nothing immoral about our teahouse.

PURDY

Then answer me this. What is bringing all that Occupation money to this particular village? There is only one thing that attracts that kind of money.

FISBY

Well, evidently there are two things.

PURDY

And if it isn't honor that you sell here, what is it?

FISBY

(Sighs unhappily)

We ... make things.

PURDY

What?

FISBY

Mats ... and hats ... and cricket cages.

PURDY

One hundred and fifty thousand yen finds its way to this village every month. You can't convince me that the American soldier is spending that much on "cricket cages."

FISBY

Well, naturally ... not all of it.

(The telephone rings. FISBY *looks at it apprehensively.)*

PURDY

Answer it.

FISBY

> (*Pauses*)

It's nothing important, sir.

PURDY

It might be for me. Answer it.

FISBY

> (*Airily*)

Oh, it rings all day, sir. Pay no attention.

PURDY

Then I'll *answer* it!

> (*He picks up the telephone.* FISBY *covers his face.*)

Hello? *What* do you want? Who is this? Well, Commander Myers, I think you have the wrong connection. This is not a brewery. Yes...yes...yes!

> (*He turns to look at* FISBY.)

Oh...I see. I see. I see.

> (*He hangs up. He turns to* FISBY, *who smiles weakly.*)

FISBY

It was the only thing we could make that anyone wanted to buy, sir.

PURDY

Brandy!

> (*Sadly*)

I don't know which is worse. Putting your country in the white slave trade or the wholesale liquor business. Congress will have to decide.

FISBY

We've the most prosperous village on the island, sir.

PURDY

This ends my Army career. I promised Mrs. Purdy I'd come out a general. You've broken a fine woman's heart, Fisby.

FISBY

You said to make the village self-supporting, sir.

PURDY

I didn't tell you to encourage lewdness and drunkenness. You've sullied the reputation of your nation and all the tears—

FISBY

All right, sir, shall I kill myself?

PURDY

Oh, don't minimize this. You don't know the enemy's genius for propaganda.

FISBY

Does anyone have to know, sir? We're doing all right.

PURDY

(*Explodes*)
Yes, they have to know! I requested an investigation myself. I've notified the Inspector General. Now I'll have to radio the whole story to Washington.

FISBY

Oh.

PURDY

(*Calmer*)
Well, what have you done with all this money you've made so dishonestly?

FISBY

Banked it in Seattle.

PURDY

Oh, that's despicable—making a personal fortune off the labor of these ignorant people.

FISBY

I haven't touched a cent for myself, sir. It's been deposited in the name of the Tobiki Cooperative. The whole village are equal partners. Share and share alike.

PURDY

(*Leaps up*)
That's *Communism!*

FISBY

Is it?

PURDY

(*Sinks down again*)
I'll be lucky to get out of this war a private.
(*He is a beaten man.*)
Well, there is only one thing for me to do.

FISBY

What is that, sir?

PURDY

First, you are to consider yourself under technical arrest. You will proceed to H.Q. at once to await court-martial.

FISBY

Yes, sir.

160

PURDY

    (Steps to the door)

Gregovich!

    (He turns back to FISBY.*)*

I must go on to Awasi this afternoon on an inspection tour. But before I leave, I intend to wipe this stain from our country's honor.

    (SERGEANT GREGOVICH *enters and salutes.*)

GREGOVICH

You called, sir?

PURDY

I did. We have some business to attend to here before going on to Awasi.

GREGOVICH

Yes, sir. I'm glad to hear it.

    (He turns to FISBY.*)*

May I congratulate you on what you've done to this village, sir. It's a dream.

FISBY

Thank you, Sergeant.

PURDY

It is an alcoholic dream. It is one vast distillery. I want you to take a detail and some axes and smash every still in this village.

GREGOVICH

Destroy them?

PURDY

Beyond repair. I want you to take another detail and rip down that teahouse.

GREGOVICH

But, Colonel—

PURDY

Pile the lumber beside the warehouse. That is an order. Do you understand?

GREGOVICH

Yes, sir!

(*As he turns to follow orders,* FISBY *sinks into his chair and the scene blacks out quickly.*)

CURTAIN

Scene 3

SCENE: *Teahouse of the August Moon.*

TIME: *A few hours later.*

AT RISE: *All the panels are down. Behind the sceens can be heard the destruction of the stills and the dismantling of the teahouse.* SAKINI *comes out from the wings and crosses down to the footlights. He flinches at the sound of an ax falling on wood.*

SAKINI
　　　(*Sadly*)
Oh, no comment.
　　　(*He walks back into the wings as all the panels are raised simultaneously. Only the frame of the teahouse has been spared. The paper panels have disappeared, the pagoda roof is gone with its tinkling bells. There are no colored lanterns and no dwarf pines to grace the path. The bare supports stand stark and ugly. Resting at the edge of the frame is a wheelbarrow.* LOTUS BLOSSOM *is collecting the last of her possessions. She takes a brass brazier down to place in the wheelbarrow. Then she stands with her back to the audience surveying all that remains of the teahouse.* FISBY *comes on, and, seeing* LOTUS BLOSSOM, *hesitates. Then he crosses to stand beside her. He takes her hand, and the two of them stand looking at the ruins.* LOTUS BLOSSOM *walks to the center of the teahouse and sits on the bare floor.* FISBY *comes up and sits on the floor facing her. She goes through the*

163

ceremony of pouring him an imaginary cup of tea. FISBY *accepts with mock formality. As he takes the cup and pretends to drink it,* LOTUS BLOSSOM *covers her face with her hands.* FISBY *sits watching her mutely.*)

SAKINI

(*Entering*)
Jeep all loaded, boss.

FISBY

I'll be along in a minute.

SAKINI

Oh, pretty soon have nice schoolhouse here.

FISBY

(*Bitterly*)
Pentagon-shaped.

SAKINI

Not be too bad. You take Lotus Blossom with you?

FISBY

No.

SAKINI

What happen to her then?

FISBY

What would have happened to her if we'd never come along?

SAKINI

Not know. Maybe someday she meet nice man and give up Geisha Guild.

164

FISBY

Ask her if there is anything I can do for her before I go.

SAKINI

(*Comes up to stand behind them*)
Nanika iitai?

LOTUS BLOSSOM

(*Softly*)
Fu-san, watashito kekkon shite chodai.

SAKINI

(*Scolding*)
Sonna bakana koto.

LOTUS BLOSSOM

(*Persistent*)
Iikara hayaku itte!

FISBY

What does she want?

SAKINI

Oh, that crazy Lotus Blossom. She want you to marry her.

FISBY

Why should she want to marry me?

SAKINI

She think you nicest man she ever see, boss.

FISBY

Tell her that I am clumsy, that I seem to have a gift for destruction. That I'd disillusion her as I have disillusioned her people.

SAKINI
  Kokai suruyo.

LOTUS BLOSSOM
  Ikitai noyo. Amerika ni. Ikitai noyo.

SAKINI
  She say she think she like to go to America. There everybody
  happy. Sit around and drink tea while machines do work.

FISBY
  She wouldn't like it, Sakini. I should hate to see her wearing
  sweaters and sport shoes and looking like an American looking
  like an Oriental.

SAKINI
  But she want to be an American, boss. She never see an American she not like, boss.

FISBY
  Some of them wouldn't like her, Sakini. In the small town where
  I live, there'd be some who would make her unhappy.

SAKINI
  Why, boss?

FISBY
  She'd be different.

SAKINI
  Dame dayo.

LOTUS BLOSSOM
      (*Takes Fisby's hand*)
  Sonna koto naiwa, Amerikatte minshu shugi desumono ne.

  166

SAKINI

She say not believe that. In America everybody love everybody. Everybody help everybody; that's democracy.

FISBY

No. That's faith. Explain to her that democracy is only a method—an ideal system for people to get together. But that unfortunately ... the people who get together ... are not always ideal.

SAKINI

That's very hard to explain, boss. She girl in love. She just want to hear pretty things.

FISBY

Then tell her that I love what she is, and that it would be wrong to change that. To impose my way of life on her.

SAKINI

Tassha dene!

FISBY

Tell her that I shall never forget her. Nor this village. Tell her that in the autumn of my life—on the other side of the world— when an August moon rises from the east, I will remember what was beautiful in my youth, and what I was wise enough to leave beautiful.

SAKINI

Issho wasurenai kara ne. Mangetsu no yoru niwa anata o omoi-dashimasu.

LOTUS BLOSSOM

(*Remains silent a moment*)

Watashi mo Fu-san no koto issho wasurenaiwa. Fu-san no koto uta ni shite, Okinawaju ni hirome masu.

SAKINI

She say she always remember you, boss. She say she guess maybe she be what she is—first-class geisha girl. She want you to know she make up long song-story about you to sing in teahouse. And maybe hundred years from now, you be famous all over Okinawa.

FISBY

> (*Rises*)

I'd like that.

LOTUS BLOSSOM

> (*Rises*)

Iinoyo. Fu-san damedemo Seiko-san ga irun dakara.

SAKINI

She say, since you not marry her, maybe you suggest somebody here.

> (FISBY *laughs.*)

She say that Mr. Seiko been looking at her like sick goat. She say what you think of him?

FISBY

Well, he took an awful beating just so he could carry her sweet potatoes.

LOTUS BLOSSOM

Fu-san, Seiko-san iito omouno?

SAKINI

She say you think she ought to marry him?

FISBY

I think she ought to decide for herself.

> (*And* MR. SEIKO *enters. He is dressed in his white suit and*

his hair is slicked down tight. He crosses to LOTUS BLOS-
SOM. *They all turn to look at him.*)

SEIKO
    (*Bows to* LOTUS BLOSSOM)
A, boku, oshimasho.

SAKINI
    (*To* FISBY)
Mr. Seiko tell Lotus Blossom he sure like to push her wheelbarrow for her.

LOTUS BLOSSOM
Iikara sakini itte chodai.

SAKINI
She say, oh, all right, but not to think that means she's his
property.
    (MR. SEIKO *beams like a schoolboy and, picking up the
handles of the wheelbarrow, he trots off stage with*
LOTUS BLOSSOM'S *possessions. She turns to* FISBY *and hands
him her fan.*)

LOTUS BLOSSOM
Korede aizu shite chodai. Soremade watashi dokonimo ikimasen
kara.

SAKINI
She say she go now, but you still her boss. She not go until you
give signal.
    (FISBY *takes the fan and puts it before his eyes. Without
waiting for him to drop it,* LOTUS BLOSSOM *runs off right.
When he lowers the fan, he knows she's gone. He sits*

169

down on the platform that had been the teahouse veranda.)
You go now, boss?

FISBY

Shortly.

FISBY

Since you not take Lotus Blossom, maybe you take me, boss?

FISBY

Major McEvoy is coming down to take charge. You'll work with him.

SAKINI

Would rather work with you.

FISBY

You'll like Major McEvoy.

SAKINI

I'll work for you for half price, boss.

FISBY

Major McEvoy will need your help in getting this village on its feet again.

SAKINI

You very hard man to bargain with, boss. If you want, I work for rice rations only.

FISBY

No.

SAKINI

You mean you going to make me work for *nothing*, boss?

FISBY

I mean *yes*, you're *not* going to work for me at all. And you belong here.

SAKINI

You know what I think happen when Americans leave Okinawa?

FISBY

What?

SAKINI

(*Grins*)

I think maybe we use pentagon-shaped schoolhouse for tea-house.

(FISBY *laughs. He gives* SAKINI *a slap on the shoulder.*)

FISBY

Good-bye, Sakini, you're a rare rascal and I'll miss you.

SAKINI

Good-bye, boss.

(FISBY *starts off left. He has gone halfway when* SAKINI *calls.*)

Boss—

FISBY

(*Stops*)

Yes?

SAKINI

You not failure.

FISBY

>   (*Laughs*)

I'll tell you something, Sakini. I used to worry a lot about not being a big success. I must have felt as you people felt at always being conquered. Well, now I'm not so sure who's the conqueror and who the conquered.

SAKINI

Not understand, boss.

FISBY

It's just that I've learned from Tobiki the wisdom of gracious acceptance. I don't want to be a world leader. I'm making peace with myself somewhere between my ambitions and my limitations.

SAKINI

That's good?

FISBY

It's a step backward in the right direction.

>   (*He throws* SAKINI *a salute.*)

Take care.

>   (*He walks off and* SAKINI *watches him go. Then, with a sigh,* SAKINI *turns to survey the skeleton of the teahouse. The silence is broken by the stormy entrance of* COLONEL PURDY.)

PURDY

Sakini! Where is Captain Fisby?

SAKINI

>   (*Points*)

Just leaving, boss.

PURDY

> (*Shouts*)

Fisby! Fisby!

> (*Gestures frantically*)

Come back here at once!

> (*He goes to the platform and sinks down gasping.*)

I'm not in shape—too much paper work.

> (FISBY *returns from the left.*)

Where in hell have you been, Fisby? I've been looking all over for you.

FISBY

I'm ready to leave, sir.

PURDY

You can't leave. You've got to stay here. You've got to help me, Fisby.

FISBY

Help doing what, sir?

PURDY

Pulling this village back together again. All hell has broken loose, Fisby.

> (*He sits down to wipe his brow.*)

Where is Gregovich!

FISBY

Breaking up the last of the stills, sir.

PURDY

Oh, *no!*

> (*He holds his head.*)

FISBY

What's happened, sir?

PURDY

I radioed the report to Washington. Some fool senator mis-
understood. He's using this village as an example of American
"get-up-and-go" in the recovery program. The Pentagon is
boasting. Congress is crowing. We're all over the papers.

FISBY

But that's wonderful, sir.

PURDY

No, it's not wonderful. A Congressional Committee is flying
over to study our methods. They are bringing in photographers
for a magazine spread. Today, Fisby, today!

FISBY

Oh, that's bad, sir.

PURDY

(*Wails*)
Gregovich!

FISBY

Isn't there any way to stall them off, sir? Quarantine the place
or something?

PURDY

You can't quarantine a congressman. They have immunity or
something.
(*He takes* FISBY *by the jacket.*)
Fisby, help me. I don't ask it for my sake. I ask it for Mrs. Purdy.
I could be a brigadier yet.
(*Before* FISBY *can answer,* GREGOVICH *comes in from the
left and salutes.*)

174

GREGOVICH

You called, sir?

PURDY

      (*Hurries over to him*)

Gregovich! Gregovich! You haven't destroyed all the stills, have you, Gregovich? No, of course you haven't.

GREGOVICH

Yes, sir, I have. I carried out orders to the letter.

PURDY

      (*Turns away shouting*)

Why can't someone disobey orders once in a while! What has happened to the American spirit of rebellion!

      (GREGOVICH *hiccups, smiles sillily and folds up on the floor.* FISBY *and* PURDY *race over to kneel beside him.*)

Sunstroke?

FISBY

Potato brandy.

PURDY

Sergeant, wake up. Do you hear me? That's an order.

FISBY

I'm afraid he's passed out, sir.

PURDY

It's desertion. I need every man. Gregovich, get to your feet!

      (*With* FISBY's *help he gets* GREGOVICH *to his feet.*)

GREGOVICH

Sorry, sir.

PURDY
I want to ask you some questions. Stop weaving.

GREGOVICH
You're weaving, sir. *I'm* perfectly still.

PURDY
You smell like a brewery.

GREGOVICH
I fell in a vat.

PURDY
You got drunk.

GREGOVICH
No, sir. I fell in a vat. Naturally, I had to open my mouth to yell for help.

PURDY
Go to the office and sober up at once.

GREGOVICH
Yes, sir.
(He salutes with a happy smile, jogs off.)

PURDY
I'm a sinking ship . . . scuttled by my own men.
(He sinks. SAKINI, who has been sitting with arms folded and a fatuous grin on his face, speaks up.)

SAKINI
Colonel Purdy?
176

PURDY

Don't bother me.

SAKINI

Stills not all destroyed.

PURDY

I haven't got time to ... What did you say?

SAKINI

We not born yesterday. Get sergeant drunk ... and give him water barrels to break.

PURDY

Sakini, my friend, you're not just saying that to make me feel better?

SAKINI

Oh, stills all good as ever. Production not cease yet.

FISBY

(*Fondly*)

You really are a rogue, Sakini.

PURDY

No ... he's really an American. He has get-up-and-go.

FISBY

Sakini, if everybody in the village worked together ... how long would it take to rebuild the teahouse?

PURDY

We don't ask the impossible.

SAKINI

Oh, maybe three minutes ... maybe five.

PURDY

That's impossible.

SAKINI

We not destroy. Just take away and hide. You watch now, boss.
(*He turns and calls.*)
Oi, mo iiyo, mo iiyo.
(*From the wings, right and left, the* VILLAGERS *step out.*)
Oi, haba, haba.
(*The* VILLAGERS *respond with happy cries and dash off.*)
Country that has been invaded many times soon master art of
hiding things.

PURDY

You think we can pull it off, Sakini?

SAKINI

You watch now.
(*And even as he speaks, the sections of the teahouse are
carried in and the swift work of putting them together
progresses before our eyes. Music is heard in the background. The pagoda roof with its tinkling bells is
lowered. The dwarf pines and the arched bridge are
brought back. The colored panels are slipped into place
and the lanterns are hung.* LOTUS BLOSSOM *comes on with
flowers which she arranges.* SAKINI *snaps his fingers and
the August moon is magically turned on in the sky. When
the final lantern is hung,* MC LEAN *comes in. He stops. His
mouth falls open.*)

PURDY

Close your mouth, Captain—haven't you ever seen a cha ya
before?
(*He turns back to* FISBY.)
Fisby, this is a land of adventure . . . a land of jade and spices . . .

of Chinese junks and river pirates.... Makes a man's blood
pound.

FISBY

Colonel ... I consider what you just said pure ...
    (*He pauses.*)
... poetry.

PURDY

Thank you ... thank you, boy.
    (*He sighs ecstatically.*)
It's the mystery of the Orient.

FISBY

It's beautiful. Simply beautiful.

PURDY

There's only one thing wrong. It needs a sign to tell people
what it is. And I think we ought to put a sign up over there
naming this Grace Purdy Avenue. And another sign ...

FISBY

Colonel Purdy. Won't you have a cup of tea?
    (*He takes his arm. As he propels him toward the tea-
    house, he speaks over his shoulder to* SAKINI.)
Twenty Star for the colonel, Sakini.
    (*As the bamboo panels begin to descend on the teahouse,*
    SAKINI *steps down to the audience.*)

SAKINI

Little story now concluded.
History of world unfinished.
Lovely ladies ... kind gentlemen—
Go home to ponder.
What was true at the beginning remains true.
Pain makes man think.

Thought makes man wise.
Wisdom makes life endurable.
Our play has ended.
May August moon bring gentle sleep.
    (*He bows*)

THE CURTAIN FALLS